Kearney/Bandley
Professional Series
Revised Edition

EVERYONE IS A CUSTOMER

By
Elizabeth I. Kearney, Ph.D.
Michale J. Bandley, Ph.D.

"It's the One Minute Manager of Customer Service"

Stewart Leonard President/CEO
Stewart Leonard's Dairy

Sterling Press

Copyright 1990 by

Michale J. Bandley
Elizabeth I. kearney
KEARNEY/BANDLEY ENTERPRISES

I.S.B.N. 0-942501-09-8

Printed in the United States of America
by Sterling Press, Provo, Utah
First Printing, 1986
Second Printing, 1987
Second Edition, 1990

Layout/Design by Analee Holden-Perica
Los Angeles, California

DEDICATION

We would like to thank our families for their willingness to rearrange their own schedules and lives during the months we worked on this book.

Without their support and caring it would have been far more difficult.

FORWARD

Chiselled in rock outside of my store in Norwalk, Connecticut, is a simple business philosophy I learned in a Dale Carnegie class many years ago,

"Rule 1: The customer is always right!
Rule 2: If the customer is ever wrong,
reread rule 1."

The point that message is making is simple, even if the customer is wrong—and it can happen—we will treat that customer as if he or she is right.

Everyone in business needs to remember that each and every customer is an asset. We estimate that the average customer spends about $100.00 per week in our dairy store , and if each one returns fifty times during the year, that means he or she is an asset worth $50,000.00 to us. Doesn't it make sense to treat such an asset as an asset. No one in business is entitled to a profit, but the customer is entitled to the best products and outstanding service. When both are delivered, profits will take care of themselves.

We believe in asking for feedback—in fact our suggestion box is our information lifeline. By ten a.m. each day all of the comments are taken out—negatives, positives, and suggestions—photocopied, and distributed to all department managers. They are also posted in employee break areas and left on tables in the employee lunchroom. We learn from these comments. Over the past few years, we have switched to combo packs of muffins—suggested by a customer—unwrapped our fish and displayed them on beds of chipped ice—a suggestion from an other customer. Every suggestion is read, considered, explored, and discussed, and within 48 hours, someone—often a member of my family—has called to thank the customer for the suggestion or comments. We value their input, and we let them know.

The authors of this book, found that those companies that have been pace setters in customer service feel as we do—the customer is the only reason we are in business. The information shared in this book was selected because it represented techniques and approaches that could be used in any company (sometimes with a little modification, sometimes with none), and the message is clear

- management must lead the way,
- build a team,
- share responsibility,

- give authority to the front line, and
- BELIEVE that it is everyone's business to make the customer happy.

I hope that as you read this book, you will learn to "think YES." After all, "You-Encourage-Support" by putting yourself ("you") in the customer's place, doing what you would want done for you, and you learn more about those wants when you "encourage" the customers to share their concerns, suggestions, and problems. In turn, management should "support" its people in "anything they do to better serve [the] customers."

The authors have put together a book that is literally the customer service version of the "One Minute Manager," it has widespread appeal. I keep this book on my desk for handy inspiration. It's the nuts and bolts of customer service.

Stew Leonard
CEO
Stew Leonard's Dairy Store

TABLE OF CONTENTS

1

WHY EVERYONE'S
A CUSTOMER

"The most important part of any business is the customer."

Michey Adza
Asst. Manager
Black Hawk Country Club

We seem to be coming full circle. The cottage industry of the late 1800's had almost disappeared, even the local mom and pop stores were fading rapidly from view by the mid 1900's. Now national reports tell us that there is an astonishing growth of small businesses, including cottage industries which are taking many forms. Entrepreneurial based companies are accounting for the largest number of employees and collectively triggering major changes.

WHY EVERYONE'S A CUSTOMER

We all know someone who has started a business, and statistics show that the survival rate of those businesses is now in favor of the person accepting the challenge. In addition, many of these companies are women-owned. Add to this number the thousands who now work from home, even though employed by large companies, and you have an important part of the workforce working out of the corporate structure—directly or indirectly.

Large companies controlled the marketplace for years, and the small companies struggled to stay alive, but now according to an article that appeared in the *Wall Street Journal*, over half of the workforce is employed in companies with fewer than 100 employees. These companies can't afford to alienate even one customer or client, and they are not isolated from the consequences of their actions as are some of the larger corporations.

Because of the small firms' ability to act quickly when they spot a market need or respond quickly when they hear of a problem, they have been giving their "big brothers" a real run for the market share. The most successful large companies have responded by revising their approach. They have instituted feed back systems, hired mystery shoppers, sent quality control experts into the field to view and review their own practices, introduced incentive programs, and even provided for employee stock options and grants whose purpose is to make each employee feel that it is truly "his or her" company and that customer satisfaction is important to "his or her" personal welfare, too. Sears, whose pay rate has never been known as one of industry's highest, has maintained a relatively stable employee base for years, and when several employees were interviewed about this, they indicated that they really were part of the company—they owned stock in it. In other words, like the entrepreneur, they had a vested interest in seeing that the marketing and service plans worked. There is no doubt that Sears has also used the entrepreneur's approach to adjusting to the competition. In 1989, they did a media blitz and closed all stores for one day to reduce prices 50%—even their detractors were swayed by this action. They stressed that they would continue putting the customer first.

"Clearly, we have a premier niche in the marketplace because all our services are focused on client needs, and we recognize that delivery and superior client value are the only services we have to offer."

R. Michael McCullough, Chairman
Booz-Allen and Hamilton

WHY EVERYONE'S A CUSTOMER

The 1970's and 1980's saw some other major changes—changes that were also triggered by customer revolt. Deregulation of the airlines, banks, trucking, and the phone company all led to the growth of new companies and problems. This was the first time that customers were given a choice about their long distance phone service, and this choice has led to a highly competitive market, markedly different pricing, a push to woo customers by stressing the response time, and improved customer service. In other words, the customers will have the last word because they always pick up the tab.

Some airlines have forgotten this. Airlines overbook, drop routes, leave late, and have merged and remerged until the general public is frustrated and angry. The problems are still with us, but there is no doubt that many are striving to impress upon the flying public that "we are concerned about you." SAS ads play this theme over and over and reinforce it with vignettes of given events. For example,

> One 1988 advertisement told about a businessman in Europe who arrived at the airport without his ticket. The ticket agent invited him to go into the lounge while she took care of the problem. She dispatched a car to the hotel where he had left the ticket, had it picked up, brought back, and got him on the plane in time.

The point being made was that

- SAS cared

- was efficient in its handling of problems—even those they did not cause.

- took the extra steps needed to insure that each and every customer was given quality service and support.

Deregulation created many problems even while it was alerting the giants to the need to respond to those served, but the competition will continue to be rough for some time to come. To some extent the customer will be the winner, but will your company be able to respond to the intense competition?

Deregulation isn't the only thing altering the market structure. An article appearing the *Wall Street Journal* on August 4, 1987, noted that there had been a decline in manufacturing and an increase in service jobs.

- Those services need to be available where and when the customer wants them.

- There needs to be greater interaction between the customer and the service provider.

- Fewer employees will be at each site so each will have to be customer-service oriented.

What will happen in your company as these changes take place? Each employee you have is literally your front line every time he/she interfaces directly, or even indirectly by billing, answering letters, or getting shipments out. What that person does can make or break that customer/company relationship. You can't afford to offer anything but the best—product or service.

For years, those working for the largest employer in the country—government, country, state, or local agencies—felt that they were not involved in customer relations. **How Untrue!** All we have to do now is look at the changing postal market to see that dissatisfaction has led to a sharp rise in competitive services. Service and speed, not cost, dictated the original shifts, and both are still major factors. More and more companies are turning to FAX machines to get their information to the other party quickly, more quickly than they could get it there by Express Mail or Federal Express. When this is coupled with the interfacing between computers and voice mail, it isn't hard to see why the U.S. Post Office instituted a customer service program several years ago.

WHY EVERYONE'S A CUSTOMER

It is time to ask yourself these questions:

- What do I offer that sets me apart from my competitors?

- What conditions within my company need to be handled in order to

  - improve service?

  - improve productivity?

  - improve profit?

- What steps am I willing and able to take to bring about the needed changes?

Write down your answers and then take notes as you go through the rest of this book. By the end of the book, you will have the information and techniques needed to take action—action that can make a major difference in your success level.

In fact, when you finish this book, you will have a blueprint for SUCCESS.

- **S** service driven
- **U** understanding customer needs
- **C** consistent service
- **C** corporate strategy planning
- **E** employee training
- **S** shopping for information
- **S** setting service goals that work.

With these elements in your success plan you will be able to move your company or organization from

- a production driven company to a customer driven one
- a solid company to a "world class" one
- a product focus to a customer focus
- a "how to" to "for you" attitude at all levels.

Marketing is going to have to change its focus. Consumers are going to take charge and may well reject manufacturers' compromises according to Laurel Cutler, vice-chairman of FCB/Leber Kastz, a New York based advertising agency and vice-president of consumer affairs of Chrysler. She also notes that marketing is going to be even more important to business success in the future. "You're (going to look) for 20% of the people who are crazy about (the product) and can't live without it, and if 80% hate it, so what." She cited the marketing approach for Absolut, as an excellent example of what can be done with a successful advertising campaign in a market where the products themselves have little, if any, real difference. "Vodka is always the most interesting example, because by law it it tasteless and odorless. So what's the difference between one vodka and another? Nothing but marketing."

The baby boomers are now moving from an era of self-indulgence and are repeating the old refrain, "Is that all there is?" Ms. Cutler says that we are seeing the maturing of America, and are now dealing with a group that understands what she calls the "banner of the Nineties," "I can't do it alone." Time is now the most scarce resource in most families, and this factor will have to be considered by those providing both products and services.

The market can be tapped to tell marketing what to do, marketing can tell operations what to produce, and strategies can be planned to tap that market and expand the need for your services or products. At every step the staff:

- must have input into the process

- must have a part in identifying and meeting the new challenge

- must be part of the solution.

At no time can you forget that your staff IS the company in the minds of your clients or customers. Keep in mind the real meaning of those two lines in the dollar sign—

—one stands for generated revenue and the other for incurred expenses, and it isn't enough to have them balance. The first must be greater than the second, and can be if you make certain that your game plan is customer driven.

KEY STRATEGY #1

YOU ARE THE KEY
TO YOUR COMPANY'S SUCCESS.

2

THE CUSTOMER REVOLT

"Customer satisfaction not only involves
assuring the quality of the production or
service provided, but also meeting the
consumer's need as an individual."

Douglas Heath
Executive Vice President
Meeting Planners International

People are the key ingredient in all human activities, yet all too often successful interaction is left to chance. In fact, it is rather like playing Russian Roulette–you have five chances to be wrong. There are six behavioral styles and multiple combinations thereof. Knowing this and using the available clues makes it possible for you to learn how to "read" your customers and clients.

Each day brings the average person into contact with numerous people–clerks, doctors, contractors, customer relations experts, etc., and conflicts arise because each person has a different view about the service or materials delivered. It is necessary to understand the signals given and be able to adjust for maximum results.

Managers know that productivity and profit are vital to the success of any company, but low morale and poor communication can sabotage a company's customer relations program and, ultimately, its growth and productivity. Different behavioral styles need to be considered since management and staff must be able to understand them in order to get the results needed.

Success is a motivator, but so is successful communication and interaction. A lack of cooperation can undermine the future of a company, so it is important to be aware of and be able to recognize, the differences among people.

No field can afford to ignore these behavioral styles!! Doctors, educators, engineers, sales personnel, consultants, and support staff all succeed in direct proportion to the attention they pay to the following system which was developed at the request of our clients.

THE "WHO'S WHO" OF
CUSTOMER RELATIONS

Everyone fits into one of six major behavioral styles, each of which has certain characteristics. All interaction is two-way, so it is also necessary to learn not only your own style but also that of others.

Carl Jung, the founder of Jungian Psychology, believed that there are basic behavioral classifications, and our research bears this out. There are six such styles—LEADERS, PERSUADERS, PATIENT PEOPLE, CAREFUL PEOPLE, RESERVED PEOPLE, AND INDEPENDENTS. These six may form many combinations, but one style generally dominates.

LEADERS: When you work with a LEADER, remember to listen more than you talk, stress results, be prepared to work hard, and be straight forward and direct. Realize that this person needs to be in control, so pressure will cost you any edge you may have. Instead, set forth well-developed alternatives and let the LEADER select from among them. It is also important to remember that this person does not have time for details. Present ONLY the "big picture" in a dignified and positive way. You may encounter a blunt, steam-roller approach–DO NOT lose your cool, APPEAR awed, or be subservient.

PERSUADERS: People-oriented individuals are easy to work with because they are friendly, outgoing, and interested in others. However, they may talk too much and not really listen. In addition, they have a tendency to jump to conclusions and be inattentive to details. They act on impulse and can be overly enthusiastic, want freedom from details, social interaction and prestige. Take time to relate to them, and–above all–be warm.

PATIENT PEOPLE:

PATIENT PEOPLE are relaxed, congenial, concerned about security, their family, and knowing all the facts. This latter trait makes them appear indecisive at times because they take time to weigh all the pros and cons. Changes threaten the status quo and tradition—both of which are important to them. Never pressure them—it would be met with resistance. Answer their questions and be prepared to take time to gather information. If you are trying to sell either an idea or a concept, realize that you will have to do so on an incremental basis.

CAREFUL PEOPLE:

CAREFUL PEOPLE are perfectionistic, open minded and

well-organized. They need to be assured of the safety of an undertaking, and when dealing with them, be accurate, concise, careful, and provide back-up data and support to assure them that—in terms of time and money—their investment is safe and will provide a good return. They are often suspicious of salesmen, and they can be both negative and dollar-prudent.

RESERVED PEOPLE:

Logic plays a major role in the lives of the RESERVED PEOPLE, and others may mistakenly feel that they are misanthropic which is not true. Unlike the PERSUADERS, this group enjoys interacting mainly with small groups or a few close friends. If you work with a reserved person, be sure that your information is presented in a straight-forward, logical, and respectful manner. Do not waste time socializing.

Stick to business, and understand that if the facts and logic lead to the conclusion you want, he/she will "sell" himself/herself. Decisions will be made ONLY after careful analysis and a thorough examination of the ideas, concepts, and details you carefully prepared. Don't be upset by blunt, unemotional responses—they are not particularly directed at you. Above all, BE BUSINESS-LIKE

**INDEPEN-
DENTS:**

INDEPENDENT PEOPLE often have a great deal of drive and ambition, but may not be interested in conforming to the rules and regulations set forth by others. In dealing with these people, remember that they are not interested in details—in fact they are bored by them. They are non-conformists (often mavericks) who enjoy attacking the system and questioning authority. You need to be prepared to cut down on details, precis your information, and never complicate an issue. The INDEPENDENT PERSON enjoys taking a risk and tackling a challenge.

They are interested in new ideas and want only the "big picture." Don't be upset if they are argumentative or DEFINITE in their statements. If what you say interests them, they will probably "buy into it" if you don't belabor the details.

THE FOUR CUSTOMER TYPES

Remember Dr. Harris' book, *I'M O.K. YOU'RE O.K.?* Well, let's use it to identify the four customer types and improve customer relations.

TYPE ONE: These people believe in themselves and accept the fact that you also have worth. Small things do not upset them and they are a delight to have as customers.

THEY RETURN TO THOSE WHO TREAT THEM WITH FAIRNESS AND PERFORM WITH SELF-ASSURANCE.

TYPE TWO: These people believe that they have value as individuals, but you don't. They have little regard for others, look out for number one, and are nice to you only as long as it is convenient. They truly need extra kindness and even compassion. They generally believe that you are wrong if there is a disagreement, and they act accordingly.

THEY DEAL WITH THOSE FROM WHOM THEY BELIEVE THEY ARE GETTING THE BEST DEAL.

TYPE THREE: No one is O.K. These people have poor self-esteem and see everything in a negative light. They have a tendency to complain about everything all of the time. In fact, they seldom trust anyone with whom they do business.

THEY COME BACK TO THE PEOPLE WHO WILL PUT UP WITH THEIR NEGATIVE BEHAVIOR AND TOLERATE COMPLAINTS BUT NOT LASH BACK AT THEM.

TYPE FOUR: These people have inferiority complexes. They feel inferior to others and believe that others do not care for them.

THEY RETURN TO BUSINESSES WHERE THE STAFF IS RESPECTFUL AND CARES.

In addition to identifying the four types of behavioral reactions, Dr. Harris also noted that we all approach our problems from one of three modes—child/parent/adult—depending upon the situation being faced. It is important to remember this and respond to clients and customers in your adult mode.

Use the following set of examples as a guide to help
you identify the mode of the person with whom you
are interacting.

Recognizing Your Customer's Mode

EXAMPLE ONE:

CHILD: "This product's a piece of junk!
I want my money back right
now!"

PARENT: "This product is not what you
advertised. I insist upon a re-
fund."

ADULT: "This calculator doesn't seem
to be working properly. Can
you fix it, get a replacement, or
arrange for a refund?"

EXAMPLE TWO:

CHILD: "Nobody pays any attention to
me. Every time I call someone
puts me on hold. I'm not going
to call anymore."

PARENT: "DON'T you put me on hold
again!! I am not going to toler-
ate this treatment."

ADULT: "I am having difficulty getting through. Would you please take my name and number and have Mr. Spillman call me back when he is less rushed?"

The customer's behavior should not influence the mode you use. Stay in your adult mod—REMEMBER, it is the only one that gets RESULTS.

Parent and child are more concerned about being right and winning, whereas the adult is only concerned with handling the situation skillfully and successfully.

Therefore, treat people fairly, give them a good deal, accept their negativity with aplomb, be respectful, and CARE.

KEY STRATEGY #2

BE A PROFESSIONAL. ADJUST TO YOUR CUSTOMERS—THEIR BEHAVIORS, THEIR NEEDS, AND THEIR WANTS.

BEHAVIORAL CLUES

Styles :	Pace:	Dress:	Wants:	Provide:
LEADER	Fast	Corporate	Results	Big Picture
PERSUADER	Fast	Fashionable	Results	Interaction
PATIENT	Unhur.	Classic	Answers	Support
CAREFUL	Consid.	Blended	Details	Facts
RESERVED	Logical	*	Logic	Direct Answer
INDEPENDENT	Fast	**	Challenge	Results

*   Like either the PATIENT or the CAREFUL person, but dresses at a given time and then forgets about it.

**   Whatever he/she pleases according to what he/she wants.

3

PUT YOURSELF IN THE CUSTOMER'S SHOES

"Business is made up of the largest group of volunteers in the world . . . customers!"

Steve Van Andel
Director/New Products
Amway Corporation

Everyone is a customer, and you should be able to easily identify with the needs noted below. You can if you will remember when you were on the "other side."

KNOW YOUR PRODUCT: Take time to learn about the product or service being offered. The customer has the right to deal with an expert.

Be able to answer the MONEY questions.

M	How MUCH is it?
O	Eliminate OBJECTIONS early.
N	Show how it fits their NEEDS.
E	EXPLAIN and expand as needed.
Y	Use the "YARDSTICK" of comparison/s.

Factually compare and contrast your service or product and your competitor's.

READ YOUR CLIENT: Determine whether your client or customer is PROCESS or RESULTS-ORIENTED. This will make a major difference in how you will present information.

The PROCESS-ORIENTED person will want to know ALL the details and have all of his/her questions answered.

The RESULTS-ORIENTED person will want you to "get to the point" and deal with the "big picture".

HAVE EMPATHY: Learn what your customer wants, identify his/her sense of urgency, and respond to it with the appropriate degree of empathy.

KNOW YOURSELF: Learn to understand your own strengths and weaknesses. Determine how you impact upon others, and learn how to adjust to the six different behavioral styles.

BE FLEXIBLE: There is no one RIGHT way to approach a situation, and if the one you are using poses a problem, CHANGE IT! Your language pattern, pace, and manner must be monitored continually to insure better communication.

BE A SELF STARTER: Take the initiative. There will be situations when it is up to you to take the first step to answer a question, respond to a problem, design a solution, or provide information.

HAVE A SENSE OF HUMOR: Remember James Thurber's definition of humor–"humor is tragedy in retrospect." Who hasn't had an embarrassing experience at which they can now laugh? Try to avoid such situations, but remember when you can't that time can change your perspective.

FOCUS ON RESULTS: Remember—the real purpose of customer relations is to insure that your customer is happy with the service, pleased with the product, and wants to return or use it again!

KEY STRATEGY #3

EACH PERSON IS UNIQUE AND SHOULD BE TREATED ACCORDING TO HIS OR HER NEEDS.

4

WHY EVERYONE'S A SALESPERSON

"In order to market a product or service, remember that the customers are king and queen. Our success is based upon quality and service to the customer. Every enterprise should have as its motto, 'Ours is the trade that service made'!"

**Meyer Fisher,President
H.B.J. Legal and Professional Pub., Inc.
d.b.a. Law Distributors**

WHO SELLS? EVERYONE!! You sell your ideas, you sell your products, you sell your services, but all too often you so it without realizing that you are in sales situations every day of your life. You NEVER stop selling, so it is essential that you realize that each of your actions impact upon others.

There is a new trend in customer relations—an awareness of the fact that it is no longer enough to provide good products and good service. We need to remember that THE PUBLIC IS THE MOST IMPORTANT INGREDIENT OF ANY BUSINESS.

Everyone in an organization deals with customers at some level, and those companies and corporations that are forging ahead are budgeting large sums for multi-level training. It is almost as if the pyramid has turned upside down–monies that used to be allocated to managerial training are now being redirected (in part) to include the entire company. For example, a communication program tailored to the executive staff has greater impact if revamped and given to all the employees, for then a change is more likely to occur.

Extensive research has identified the steps to take to achieve successful customer relations and ways to insure that those relationships don't flounder and fail.

STEPS TO SUCCESS

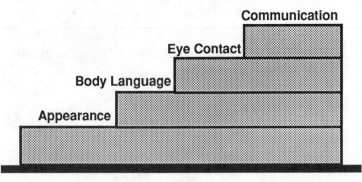

1. **APPEARANCE** is a critical factor since it makes a statement. Be sure that the statement you make is the one you want to make. When you mirror your client's and customer's dress and/or behavior, you and your ideas are more likely to be accepted because you will relate better to them. You come as a package–hair, nails, grooming, and condition of dress all need to be attractive, appealing, and interesting.

2. **BODY LANGUAGE** affects the subconscious, and the subconscious is where decisions are made. Therefore, you need to monitor not only the words you use, but your body language as well since you are often treated according to your non-verbal signals.

3. Experts teach that **EYE CONTACT** is important, and even those who play it down agree that one does need to look squarely at the person–at least part of the time–while talking.

4. **COMMUNICATION** bridges must exist before any real interaction can occur. This means that semantics (your selection of words) and listening are two of the major areas that must be considered and utilized.

WHAT TO DO

1. Make eye contact.
2. Smile.
3. Be subtle
4. Be interested in the client.
5. Respond positively.
6. Consider your dress.
7. Keep your cool.
8. Follow-up.
9. Listen.
10. Build rapport.

Make certain that the other person understands what you are saying. Good salespeople know that until the other person hears what you have to say, you have not really communicated. Give the other person your total attention, build rapport, and realize that your success–and that of your company–depends upon your ability to sell your ideas, products, and/or services. You need to make certain that customers want to come back because they enjoy working with you and know that their needs will be met.

KEY STRATEGY #4

YOU NEVER STOP SELLING: IDEAS, SERVICES, OR PROUCTS, AND YOUR COMMUNICATION CAN DETERMINE YOUR SUCCESS.

5

YOUR ATTITUDE MAKES THE DIFFERENCE

"My attitude is my choice. I can not change my would or my surroundings, but I can change my attitude about them."

Peter G. Thomas
Chairman of the Board
Century 21 Real Estate

You are the key to the success of your company's relations with customers and clients!! You are the bridge between the customer and the company; between the customer and the problems; between the customer and the sale. Your most important goal is to satisfy the customer, and your **ATTITUDE** will play a major role in developing this satisfaction.

QUESTION ONE: What are the most crucial aspect of customer relations?

This question produced attitude-related information which indicated that those surveyed were most pleased when those in the company:

- were personable
- were results-oriented
- put the customer first
- cared
- were courteous
- were well-informed
- were considerate
- were sincere
- were understanding

- were sociable
- had a sense of humor
- were direct, but not rude
- were patient
- were honest
- were sensitive

Do you think that your customer is important? Your view will come across in your attitude which is reflected through the behaviors noted above.

Let's check your attitude. Respond to the following statements by marking the appropriate column.

Attitudinal Checklist

	Always	Usually	Seldom
1. I try to remain positive.			
2. I see problems as challenges.			
3. I like myself and others.			
4. I "go the extra mile."			
5. I enjoy people.			
6. I'm sensitive to other's needs.			
7. I try to look at situations from all points of view.			
8. I am results oriented.			
9. When appropriate, I have a sense of humor.			
10. I'm patient.			
11. I put the customer first.			
12. I strive to be courteous at all times.			
Totals			

SCORING INSTRUCTIONS: Give yourself 10 points for every check in the "always" column; 6 points for the "usually" column; and 1 point for each check in the "seldom" column.

If you have 90 to 100 points, your attitude is a positive asset, and you are productive.

If your score was 80 to 89, your attitude is generally positive, but may not be consistently so.

If your score is below 80, you may want to reassess your behaviors and make some changes.

YOU CHOOSE YOUR ATTITUDE

William James (the father of psychology) said, "People can alter their lives by altering their attitudes," and Dale Carnegie made a fortune by designing programs to help people do just that. Failure is avoidable! Those who see obstacles as roadblocks fail!! Those who see them as stepping stones succeed!!

Marilyn Van der Bur, a motivational speaker, tells a story about a well-known public figure. You may recognize her.

> While still a teenager, this woman decided that she wanted to be an actress. She moved to New York where she applied to a famous drama school and was turned down. She tried another with the same results. She then sought a job as a dancer, got one in a chorus line only to become ill. Pride kept her from asking for help from home, but because therapy was needed, she had to return home. Once recovered, she headed to Hollywood for a fresh start. After serving a long period as an apprentice (starlet), she got her first good role as she neared 40–the year she had her first child.

This woman certainly was not an "overnight" success, was she? Few would fail to recognize her name. Lucille Ball.

Her attitude was the key, and many of our successful clients request that attitude and techniques for changing it be addressed during our seminars on various topics. They have found attitude is the key to job satisfaction, customer satisfaction, and productivity because someone with a positive attitude is more open to suggestions and change.

KEY STRATEGY #5

YOU ARE IN TOTAL CHARGE OF YOUR ATTITUDE, WHICH IN TURN SHAPES YOUR LIFE.

6

HOW YOUR SELF ESTEEM
AFFECTS THE SALE

"We have to continually demonstrate and convey a responsive, efficient, and concerned awareness of the customer's needs—a willingness effectively communicated to help the customer be more successful."

Sy Graff
Vice President
Special Service Administration

Self-esteem is a quiet sense of self-respect and self-worth, and when it is deep-seated you are glad you are you! With high self-esteem you do not waste time or energy trying to impress others. You KNOW that you have value as a person.

Self-esteem is the mainspring of success and the lack of it is the cause of most human failure. Where do we get it, and how do we keep it? The basis of a good feeling of self-worth begins in childhood. A strong feeling of self-respect is based on the conviction that you are lovable and matter because you exist and because you are worthwhile.

You have the need to feel lovable and worthy, and these needs do not end with childhood–they are with you until death. It is essential that these needs be met, just as essential as it is to have air to breathe and food to eat. The ONLY person you can't avoid is you!! The most important ingredient in mental health— and often physical health—is a good sense of self-esteem. Where do we get it? It is not related to wealth, education, geography, or social class. It comes from the quality of relationships—including your relationship with yourself.

Realize that your feeling of self-worth impacts upon every aspect of your life including your ability to relate to your colleagues and your customers or clients. Your own productivity, success, and attitude all relate to this feeling.

React to the following statements:

	YES	NO
1. I enjoy getting up in the morning.	___	___
2. I am usually in a good mood.	___	___
3. Most people like me.	___	___
4. I'm energetic.	___	___
5. I'm basically an optimist.	___	___
6. I can laugh at my own mistakes.	___	___
7. Those I care about value my opinion.	___	___
8. I am my own best friend.	___	___
9. I am still growing and changing.	___	___
10. I am not afraid to express my views.	___	___

Give yourself ten points for every "yes" answer. If you score between 90 to 100 points, you have excellent self-esteem.

If you score between 80-89, you have good self-esteem, but a little improvement is needed.

If your score is between 70-79, you should begin to take some positive steps that would make a difference in you life.

A score of 60-69 could mean that your lack of self-esteem is "dragging you down." Are you ready to make a positive change?

IMPROVING SELF-ESTEEM

There are certain natural laws of behavior which influence self-esteem and reshape and remold our lives and behavioral patterns if we choose. Most of us voice a desire to change, but do not take the necessary steps to accomplish it. When we wish for something it seldom comes into existence. The same is true when we want it, but when we NEED it, we generally take steps to get it. What this means to us is that until we really feel that our life is less fulfilling and rewarding without the desired level of self-worth, we will probably do nothing about it.

Once there is a need to change, the following approaches can be used:

DESIGN A GAME PLAN

Generalities rarely result in success. With specifics there is rarely failure. Goals help us establish control over our time and lives. Success builds on success, so you should establish short term goals as well as long-range ones. Keep in mind that your game plan should contain a design for interfacing effectively with your clients and customers.

TAKE CHARGE OF YOUR ATTITUDE

You choose your attitudes, and they shape your life. They make a difference in

- how others react to you.

- whether you can learn from your mistakes.

- whether you can accept the change that is basic to today's world.

- whether or not you believe that you can succeed.

- your drive to succeed.

- your willingness to forgive and/or understand yourself and others.

Reinhold Neibur gave excellent advice when he said, "God grant me the serenity to accept the things I cannot change, the courage to change the things I can, and the wisdom to know the difference." This quotation is used as the motto in many organizations today to emphasize the importance of continually building one's self-esteem.

Many of the consequences of low self-esteem are seen in the statistics related to suicide, child abuse, mental abuse, drug abuse, and obesity.

COUNTERACTING LOW SELF-ESTEEM

- Set goals.

- Be your own best friend.

- Eat properly.

- Build on your strengths.

- Give to others.

- Reward yourself.

- Offset your weaknesses.

- Improve your appearance.

- Get out of your comfort zone!

The negative impact of low self-esteem on business success has led corporations and companies to hire outside consultants to design and present programs tailored to the personal needs of the employees.*

* About 30% of our business in the past has dealt with this problem.

KEY STRATEGY #6

DESIGN A SELF-ESTEEM GAME PLAN WHICH INCLUDES POSITIVE STEPS TO MAXIMIZING YOUR IMPACT!

7

TELEPHONE PERSUASION

> "People buy from people . . . people they like, they trust, they respect; no one buys from an enemy."

> **Howard G. Seebach**
> **Sales Manager**
> **Dupont**

The phone can be your most important tool or your greatest enemy, depending upon how you use it. According to our clients, everyone from the CEO to the switchboard operator needs to understand the importance of the telephone techniques.

THE TEN UNWRITTEN RULES

1. You are your company's representative, and this means that you need to BE PROFESSIONAL AT ALL TIMES. Make a commitment to excellence, and then make certain that your language conveys this fact.

2. It is also important to **USE COMMON SENSE.** Many problems can be solved if you use common sense and then tailor your response to the behavioral style of the client, customer, or organizational member.

3. A great deal can be learned by really **LISTENING** to the tone, pause pattern, language pattern auditory, visual, or feeling) and emotional level of the person.

4. Remember to **BE DIPLOMATIC** because abrasiveness is always counterproductive and promotes a bad company image as well as a negative counter attack in many instances.

5. It is important to **UNDERSTAND THE COMPANY POLICY** and make certain that you know and support the company's rules, policies and traditions. Be careful not to present it in such a way as to irritate others to whom it may not be of prime importance.

6. Make it a point to **TAKE AN INTEREST IN OTHERS.** People know when you are genuinely interested in them, and it makes a difference in their reactions and the resultant relations established.

7. **DON'T TRUST YOUR MEMORY.** Take notes on what has been said or promised, and then make certain that you follow through on any promises made or questions asked. Remember you ARE the company as far the client or customer is concerned.

8. **MAXIMIZE YOUR IMPACT.** Remember that the first two words of any phone conversation are considered "give away" words and that a professional approach is always appreciated.

9. **BE COURTEOUS** and remember to provide your name and number. Others are upset when you don't because they are more comfortable with the "known" than with the "unknown."

10. **TONE SETS THE STAGE,** and others not only react to it but mirror it. Many companies are now providing staff training that stresses keeping a "smile in your voice." In fact, it is so important that some companies are putting mirrors on desks and asking their employees to look in them while talking on the phone. You might also want to tape the same statement two times—once while looking in a mirror and smiling and once while frowning. Listen to the tape and note the difference. Gladys Nicastro, a well-known consultant in this field, said, "The face you see in the mirror is the voice they hear."

ANSWERING THE CALL

ANSWER PROMPTLY

Pick up the call after two rings, but always before the fourth. Have your pencil and paper ready. Don't keep the client waiting.

IDENTIFY YOURSELF

Never assume your voice will be recognized. Identify yourself, the department and the company. If it is not your call, identify for whom you are making it.

HAVE A FRIENDLY MANNER

Show your interest and set the pattern for the rest of the conversation. Try to keep background noises down if possible.

AVOID THE HOLD BUTTON

Avoid putting the client or customer or client on hold if at all possible. If you must do so, KEEP IT BRIEF.

DON'T PLAY PASS AROUND

People get frustrated when they are transferred from place to place. Ask permission to make the transfer and give the name and extension number of the party to whom the call is being transferred. Then, if they need to call back or get cut off, they know how to get back to the right party.

GIVE FEEDBACK

Feedback reinforces what has been said and gives you the data needed to follow-through appropriately. Besides, it lets the other person know that you heard and are concerned enough to take note of his/her needs or concerns.

PERSONALIZE THE CONVER-SATION

Find out the person's name and USE it. To most people, their name is one of the most important things in their world.

SIX STEPS TO TELEPHONE TACT

There are certain steps to telephone tact, and when they are used, you are in a much better position with your customer or client.

1. **KEEP YOUR VOICE PLEASANT**. Practice on a tape recorder. Voices can be changed with practice.

2. **BE COURTEOUS.** Remember to behave as though "the customers are always right." Treat them as V.I.P.s.

3. **EVERY CALL IS IMPORTANT**. Even if you don't see the call as a high priority one, don't forget that the client does.

4. **MIRROR LANGUAGE PATTERNS.** Communication is enhanced when both parties speak the same "language" (feeling, auditory, or visual). Also, avoid substandard usage.

5. **BE POSITIVE.** Your attitude often makes a difference in the response you get. Control your attitude and don't let the attitude of others affect you negatively.

6. **ADMIT WHEN YOU ARE WRONG.** Most people understand and are more willing to be cooperative if you explain the situation in a sincere, courteous way.

You can present a positive company image, turn problem callers into satisfied customers, and gain their trust when you use the right telephone techniques.

> # KEY STRATEGY #7
>
> ## YOUR PHONE RELATIONS PROJECT YOUR COMPANY'S IMAGE!

8

LISTEN TO THE CUSTOMER

"Listening is the absolute key to identifying and serving customer needs."

Manny Steil
President
Communication Development, Inc.

More and more attention is being given to the part that listening plays in the total communication process. Research studies, articles, and books are bringing the subject to the forefront as an identified key to success.

Although we spend approximately 45% of our communication time listening, 30% speaking, 16% reading, and 9% writing, schools seldom offer training in this area. Listening comprehension can be improved by 25% (or more) if you develop active listening language (the three "languages" will be discussed later in this chapter).

An increasing number of companies are now providing training in the area of listening skills. It has been proven that one of the greatest barriers to sales is the inability to "really" listen. One of the greatest problems faced in inter-office and intra-office communication is the failure of one person to comprehend what the other REALLY said.

What are the barriers to listening and what can be done to overcome them?

LISTENING BARRIERS

There are eight major barriers to listening.

- CULTURAL
- MOTHER TONGUE
- LISTENING LANGUAGE
- SOCIAL
- EDUCATIONAL
- ATTITUDINAL
- VALUES
- SEXUAL

These barriers must be removed before there can be interactive listening for rapport and good customer relations. The steps for removing them are listed below:

LISTEN BEFORE YOU SPEAK and avoid snap judgments or dogmatic statements.

REPEAT THE MESSAGE to ensure understanding—yours and theirs.

MAKE LISTENING A DUAL RESPONSIBILITY of both speaker and listener.

- Speakers should make their points and purposes clear and use effective materials to hold the attention and interest of the listeners.

- Listeners need to be actively involved in the informational interchange.

CONTROL NEGATIVE PHYSICAL FACTORS such as noise, poor acoustics, gloomy room atmosphere, uncomfortable furniture, and poor voice projection.

These techniques can be developed if there is a desire to do so, and the habits that have been identified as the most irritation ones can be eliminated or reduced with thought and practice. A survey of customers revealed that the following actions were the most irritating.

They are the most likely to create customer relations problems. Are you guilty of any of these?

"The service department rep *didn't even bother to hear me out.*"

"My dentist's receptionist *interrupts me* every time I call in to get help."

"The clerk at my credit union *hasn't smiled* since the day I became a member."

"I never shop at Wrinkles Department Store anymore because the sales staff always *talked down to me.*"

"I think we are losing business because my manager *never looks at* our customers when they come in to talk to him."

"I hate trying to explain things to my insurance agent. He always *interrupts me and puts words* in my mouth."

"Nothing irritates me more than to finish an explanation and then have the person to whom I am speaking ask questions that show he/she *wasn't listening.*"

"I've quit going to restaurants where the waiter and waitresses *ignore me.*"

The situations above have elements in common–the problems could have occurred in any business, and the customers or clients were the losers in the short run, but in the long run, the business will suffer.

MAKE IT A LISTENING MATCH

You can ensure that both the business and the customer or client are winners by tailoring your information to their listening style and listening language. Everyone perceives the work through his/her basic sense–sight, sound, or feelings. In each person, one of these senses becomes dominant and influences comprehension patterns—even the listening language. Once the style is identified, there will be less of a gap between what is said and meant and what is heard and reacted to.

It is possible to identify an individual's listening language by noting the words which are used. Those who are **VISUALLY ORIENTED** will make extensive use of words that relate to "seeing" their world and its elements; those who are **AUDITORY** will illustrate the fact by extensive utilization of "hearing" words, and those who are **FEELING** will reveal it though the use of words that relate to emotions.

VISUAL: It is not hard to tell that Mr. Virgil is a **VISUALLY ORIENTED** person when he walks into your office and says, "Would you please **look** at this report? I can't **imagine** how anything with so many errors could get past your proof reader. I thought that I made it quite **clear** that market **focus** demanded accuracy." Even though he delivered this with a smile, there was no question about his irritation.

AUDITORY: On the other hand, the same proof reader goofed when Miss Drake's materials were prepared, and she lets your know. "I can not believe that I didn't make myself **heard** when I **told** your agent what I needed. She apparently **tuned me out**, because if she had **listened**, she would have been able to

tell that this was wrong." Miss Drake is obviously **AUDITORY.**

FEELING: After dealing with Miss Drake and Mr. Virgil, you would think that you had handled every possible style, but there is still another one, **FEELING.** Miss Archer marches into your office upset and in tears. She has had a real problem **getting a handle** on her **feelings** after all the **effort** she had to put in on this project. She doesn't want to **hurt** the feelings of the young lady who handled her order. She just can't **understand** how anyone could make such a mistake—three pages were left out.

What does all this mean? Well, it means that if you are to ensure communication, you are going to have to note the clue words (see **bold words** in the sections above) and respond using those words or similar ones.

The VISUAL person hears best when a response begins with visual word such as "see," "Illustrate," "look," "design," 'focus," "draw," or "chart."

The **AUDITORY** person registers auditory words best and is more receptive when words such as "hear," "listen," "tell," 'speak," "voiced," or "comment" are used.

On the other hand, the **FEELING PERSON** is most responsive when words such as "relate," "interact," "comfortable," or "ambiance" are employed.

Although it is not necessary to totally change your own style, it is important to concentrate on the words being used as well as the message being conveyed. You can jot down some of the key words and play them–or their counterparts–back for more effective communication. After all, the phone carries no sound until you connect with the other party, and the same is true of communication.

KEY STRATEGY #8

**MIRROR THE CLIENT'S
LISTENING LANGUAGE,
(VISUAL, AUDITORY, OR FEELING),
FOR THE BEST RESULTS.**

9

WORDS AREN'T ENOUGH

"Public education is a product-oriented business, and we need to merchandise better what we do as teachers and what students do as learners."

Ramon C. Cortines
Superintendent
San Francisco Unified School District

We have ONLY four minutes to make an impression on the other person, for people rely more on what they see and what you do than on the words you use.

The well-known UCLA study showed that

> 7% of the impact comes from the words said,
> 38% of the impact relates to the body language, and
> 55%of the impact is related to the way you say the words.

This information is important to remember whenever you are dealing with a customer. For example, there is a story that came out of WWI about an army meeting held by a young sergeant who was asking his men to enroll in a life insurance program set up by the army. He told them that by doing so they would be providing for their families in case death. The men showed no interest in it even though he pointed out that their money would vest and the rates were exceptional. After several tries, he gave up. A young officer saw his disappointment and asked if he could talk. "Now, look here men, here's the deal. The army is offering us $10,000 life insurance policies before we get to the front. If we die, it costs them money. Who are they going to put on the front lines—the man that is going to cost them $10,000 dollars or a man who doesn't cost them a cent?" After a shocked silence, every man in the room signed up! Why? The approach had impact!!!

When you gear your information to the behavioral and values styles of the customers addressed, you increase its impact and its likelihood of acceptance. Our clients have found that this approach increases productivity and profit!

Good customer relations require that you understand the other person. They are more likely to develop when we are friendly—but not overly so; when we are at ease and comfortable with the other person; and when we are assertive, but not aggressive. Pay attention to your own nonverbal signals. They may have more impact than you realize.

Eye contact is critical. How often do you look away? Where do you look—up, off to the side, or at the person? By using your powers of observation, you can pick up signals from your client. All of us can spot the signals that signify rejection—the person looks away, rolls his/her eyes, begins to squint. When we see these signals, we get the message.

You can control eye contact.

> **One**—observe;
> **Two**—synchronize, and
> **Three**—lead.

Pay attention to your customer's eye movements. If you find that they are frequently focused away from you, don't try to force contact. Look away as often as the customer does. Gradually increase the contact by looking at the customer for longer periods of time. We have been taught that those who look at us are more concerned, interested, and honest than others. Use this past information to your advantage and build the rapport you need.

Gestures are an important way to convey our information and personalize our communication. Open hands with palms up seem to say "trust me," whereas, fists and fidgeting fingers often make the client or customer feel uncomfortable and ill-at-ease. When people put their hands on their hips, they assume a power position. EVEN THOUGH BODY LANGUAGE IS IMPORTANT, DON'T READ MORE INTO IT THAN WAS THERE! For example, arms crossed across the chest are often thought to indicate hostility or doubt. The person could just be cold.

A study done by Dr. Edward Hall produced interesting anthropological information that affects our communication in many ways that most of us don't consider. We have envelopes of space (a personal space that is not to be invaded except by invitation). The space you maintain—and the space that your customers or clients prefer to have maintained between them and others—makes a marked difference in the quality of communication used. For example:

DISTANCE	TYPE OF COMMUNICATION
18 inches	Intimate
1 to 2 feet	Personal
2 to 4 feet	General Contact
4 to 7 feet	Social
7 to 12 feet	Formal
more than 12 feet	Public

When this distance is violated, the interchange is often short-circuited. We have all seen someone backing away from another who is moving forward, talking, and unaware that little, if any, REAL communication is occurring.

The space envelope is less developed to the side and back. If you aren't sure that this is right, try this experiment. Get in a crowded elevator and face the group. Watch the reaction!!

YOUR VOICE
MAKES A DIFFERENCE

People form a lasting impression of you from hearing you speak. Make certain that the impression is a good one. The variation of pitch can create different moods and reactions, so you can control the impact you make by controlling pitch of your voice.

Accents and language patterns can help or hurt communication. If your pattern is the same as the customer's, you are on firm ground. However, some patterns are irritating to those from other geographical areas. Remember this, and avoid the most pronounced patterns of colloquialisms. Enunciate clearly; blurred words can be annoying and confusing.

Your voice resonates differently in your head than it comes across to others, so tape yourself and play the tape back with the intent of improving your voice pattern and tone. Remember to pause when you are searching for words or ideas. Don't fill in the pauses with "you know's" and "uh's."

Usually, the most pleasant voice to listen to is low in pitch. Your customers/clients will listen longer if your voice is soothing and not penetrating, so work on keeping it pitched low even when irritation or frustration rises. Most people associate a high pitch with hysteria.

Working on your voice can be fun!! Try it.

KEY STRATEGY #9

FOUR MINUTES IS ALL YOU HAVE TO MAKE A FAVOR- ABLE IMPRESSION ON YOUR CUSTOMER, CLIENT, OR COLLEAGUE.

10

GAMES CUSTOMERS PLAY

"Don't ever forget that anything anybody can get from us they can probably get from somebody else and maybe even better."

Mike Welch
President
Credit Union Executives Society
Madison, Wisconsin

How you deal with games customers play is often the determining factor in your success. The reason people play games is as varied as the people themselves, but you need to be able to respond appropriately no matter what the reason.

What are some of the games? They are easy for you to spot, for they seem to fall into certain patterns.

1. "Poor me."
2. "But you promised . . ."

3. "Your salesman promised me . . ."
4. "Go ahead, everyone kicks me when I'm down anyway."
5. "I can get it for less down the street."
6. "I have never been so insulted in my whole life."
7. "I can't believe this. My neighbor, Mr. Chairman of the Board will be quite interested to hear about this."

Once you have spotted the pattern, what do you do? Well, the first thing to do is to remember that each of the above games hides the real agenda. If you buy into any one of these, then you are unable to do your job effectively or service the customer's real needs. Let's look at a few of the above and design a game plan.

"IF YOU LIKE ME, YOU WOULD FIX IT FOR ME."

REAL PROBLEM: This person is a manipulator, and the real goal is control, not repair.

ONE SOLUTION: Empathize without letting the situation build. "What would you like to see done to resolve the problem?"

"POOR ME."

REAL PROBLEM: The customer can't cope and wants you to step in as "parent."

ONE SOLUTION: Give some "how to" advice; suggest the steps that can be taken to solve the problem. "Here, you can follow this guide sheet, and it will tell you just what to do."

"GO AHEAD, EVERYONE KICKS ME WHEN I'M DOWN ANYWAY."

REAL PROBLEM: Low self esteem. This person expects to be mistreated. Don't oblige.

ONE SOLUTION: Don't buy in—use techniques that will build the customer's self-confidence. "Look, these things happen to all of us. Let's see how we can make certain that it doesn't happen again."

"I CAN GET IT FOR LESS
DOWN THE STREET."

REAL PROBLEM: This person is a bargain hunter—quality and service are less important than price.

ONE SOLUTION: Do a comparative analysis for the customer, being certain to include all the variables involved. Price is only one.

I HAVE NEVER BEEN SO INSULTED
IN MY WHOLE LIFE.

REAL PROBLEM: False pride and dignity are the real problems here. The person wants, and may need, special attention.

ONE SOLUTION: If possible, provide something special—a newer item, a larger version, or one-on-one service.

YOUR SALESMAN PROMISED ...

REAL PROBLEM: A desire to play one against the other for personal benefit is the real problem.

ONE SOLUTION: Agree up to a point. "I don't blame you for being upset if you get conflicting stories. I guess he should have referred you to sections in the brochure instead of just handing it to you."

"I CAN'T BELIEVE THIS.
I SHALL HAVE TO LET MY NEIGHBOR
—MR. CHAIRMAN OF THE BOARD—
KNOW ABOUT THIS!"

REAL PROBLEM: An independent who doesn't believe that rules apply to him/her.

ONE SOLUTION: Let this person know that you would work things out if you could.

It is important to remember to back up and address the problem, not the symptom. Recognize the cause and treat that. With practice, it is easy to identify the game, identify the real problem, and solve it.

KEY STRATEGY #10

**YOU CAN'T RESPOND UNTIL
YOU KNOW THE MESSAGE;
LEARN TO RECOGNIZE
THE GAMES CUSTOMERS PLAY.**

11

DEALING WITH ANGER

"The customer may not always be right, but he's always the customer. Your job is to help him identify his need and show him how your product or service can meet his need."

James B. Jacobson
Executive Vice President CalFed Inc.
-and-
Chairman of the Board
Beneficial Standard Life Insurance Company

Irate customers are a fact of life although we all wish we didn't have to face them. No matter how diligently we try to conduct our business, there are those who feel that they did not get what was promised, what they paid for, or the service that was needed. When customer complaints do arise, the issue of who is to blame should not be the major factor. What is really needed is a solution to the problem in order to bring about customer satisfaction. After all, return business is the key to success for most companies.

People go through distinct stages before anger strikes, and those phases are fairly easy to identify.

> •DISAPPOINTMENT is often voiced through such phrases as "perhaps you are not aware" or "maybe your office didn't get my letter." Effective handling of the customer defuses the situation at this level. Realize that this is a signal, and take the problem seriously. Seek a resolution.

> •FRUSTRATION is often the next stage, and the shrill voice is often a clue. Anger is building. Do everything possible to head off the fury that may follow.

> •ANGER is the third stage of this pattern, and at this point, the client or customer is out of control.

First, hear the problem through, and avoid the impersonal approach. For example, you may need to fill out a form that requires everything from the social security number to the birthdate, but take a minute first to let them know that you plan to help and are empathetic. Then go into the request for information after explaining that it will be needed and why.

Relate to the customers where they are; don't ever appear to be talking "down to them." With rapport, you gain trust and are on your way to cooperation and resolution.

DEALING WITH DIFFICULT PEOPLE

Let the irate person blow off steam. Like the hot air balloon, anger can only stay afloat as long as there is heat. After the pressure is released, you will be better able to handle the complaints. The concepts we share with our clients make the difference between positive and negative customer relations.

FIRST, you need to use The Conflict Formula.

- Keep an open mind.
- Listen to the problem.
- Stay in the adult mode.
- Gather information that is needed.
- Let others vent their frustrations.
- Determine the "real" source of the conflict.
- Evaluate the outcome to all concerned.
- Remain objective and calm.

Successful negotiators exist in every walk of life, and they succeed because they really listen to the other person–not just the words spoken, but the intent of those words, as well. They also control their own re- actions and base their decisions on facts–not emo- tions. These factors, coupled with their ability to see all sides of an issue and work toward a win/win solution, insure their success.

After that you can move into the resolution stage and negotiate a solution. This will require that you

ASK questions that will help you understand the real problem. You may wish to use the 5 W's and 1 H (who, what, where, when, why, and how).

DETERMINE how to present the proposed solution. If the person is results-oriented, state the big picture; if process-oriented, give details.

CONSIDER all possible outcomes and propose a solution.

PRESENT the proposal to the customer, and ask if it would be satisfactory. If not, ask what would be acceptable.

CONSIDER the customer's proposed solution in light of company policy. If it falls within the scope of that policy and you have the authority to grant it, go his/her way. If you don't, perhaps your boss could. It is always best to act as quickly as possible.

REALIZE that if the proposed solution does not conform to the policy, the situation should be explained and steps taken to satisfy the customer.

What if there is no apparent solution to the problem? You have tried every road and found them all blocked. Level with the customer. Tell him/her how frustrated you are and explain that you will try some other avenues and then get back to him/her with what you have learned. The worst that could happen is that there are no avenues to follow, and the best is that time may solve the problem.

Even in such an instance, COURTESY IS OF PRIME IMPORTANCE. Courtesy goes by many names— politeness, concern, manners, charm, tact, diplomacy—but no matter what it is called, it is still the crux of business success just as it was 100 years ago. In fact, many companies are now realizing that one-on-one service and concern is the basis of successful business in the latter part of the 20th Century. Large hotels are now striving for the personal touch, and major corporations have realized the focus MUST be on the individual. COURTESY is the key to that focus.

KEY STRATEGY #11

EVERYONE GETS ANGRY. IT'S HOW YOU DEAL WITH IT THAT MATTERS!

12

STRATEGIES
OF NEGOTIATION

"Just as you can gain some of the greatest insights into people by the little things that they say and do, it is the little things you say and do that often make the most enriching impression."

Mark H. McCormack
President
International Management Group

People used to think that negotiations were only important in labor relations or diplomacy, but the fact is that we negotiate for everything we want and do it daily. Give and take is part of our world, and all of our transactions involve negotiating. So it isn't whether we do or do not use negotiation skills–but rather how well!!

In all aspects of business, customer relations included, we need to remember that building more profitable relations mean greater success, and skilled, successful negotiators are trained, not born.

Think of yourself as a negotiator. What do you need to know and remember?

1. BE PREPARED

Nierenberg says, "Preparation can make an amateur negotiator look like a pro."

BE CERTAIN you have your facts at hand. "The worst time to lean new facts is when the negotiation is in progress." Also, never allow the customer to be your only source of information.

2. UNDERSTAND THE CUSTOMER'S STYLE

There are six different behavioral styles. Be able to identify each and respond accordingly (See Chapter 2).

3. UNDERSTAND ALL OPTIONS

You can use the same techniques over and over, but they won't always come out the same. So, you need to know when to change your approach.

4. **RECOGNIZE THE REAL AGENDA**

Find out what the other person wants—even if it isn't put into words. Make it A WIN/WIN SITUATION.

5. **USE SILENCE**

Silence is power. Most people hate silence and fill the void which may well give you the information needed to move ahead.

First, YOU PROBABLY HAVE MORE POWER THAN YOU THINK YOU DO!!

- You know the product and its value.
- You have a team to back you up.
- You have the ability to use words to soothe.
- You are the only one in control of your emotions.

Second, YOU CAN'T HIT A TARGET UNLESS YOU SET IT!!

- Preplan and preplay.
- Have a game plan for all contingencies.
- Expect to succeed.
- Know your options—whom can you call for help and support?

Third, YOU CAN BREAK DEADLOCKS!!

- Use the behavioral motivators that fit the behavioral styles.
- Stay in your adult mode.
- Use the correct listening language (auditory, visual, or feeling)

Fourth, HELPFUL CONCESSIONS CAN'T HURT YOU!!

- Pace yourself to the other person.
- Split the differences when appropriate.
- Make certain that both the company and the customer "win."

Remember that often "just recognizing a tactic will neutralize it." For example, "realizing . . . that the other side is attacking you personally in order to impair your judgment may well frustrate the efforts," according to Roger Fisher and William Ury in their book, *Getting to Yes.*

The most important elements you bring to any exchange are your own goals and the goals of your organization, but you need to understand that "to some skilled bargainers, negotiation is a game." Those who have the rules of give and take down pat get more than they give. Be certain that you are not letting others write the "rules of your game." It is true that in business everything is negotiable, but if you are prepared to present reasons for the favorable position you seek and the rationale for your criteria, you will give your goals integrity, and your argument will be far more persuasive.

KEY STRATEGY #12

TAKE A POWER POSITION AND THEN NEGOTIATE FOR A WIN/WIN SOLUTION!

13

A CREATIVE APPROACH TO CUSTOMER RELATIONS

"When you assess all of your priorities, the one you can't neglect is customer service. That's wy our company motto is 'Customer Service Comes First'."

Tom Griffin
Prisident
Coldwell Banker

When creativity is your calling card, you have a dynamite way to insure the success of your ideas, products, and services. What used to work is no longer working, and the companies that are moving ahead in the competitive race are those that have faced this fact and are doing something to spark the creative process in their most important asset–you. It doesn't matter what your title is, what your function is, or who you are. What does matter is that you bring creativity to the work process.

A famous woman executive was interviewed recently and noted that she believed in cost-of-living raises, but would never give a promotion nor a raise to anyone who was still doing the job in the same way that it had been done when the person was hired. The reaction to this is mixed, but consider it. You will see that what she really means is that stagnation should not be rewarded. How would you do in her company?

First, you need to realize that not all creativity involves producing a piece of art, designing a building, nor preparing a new approach to a scientific problem. You can be creative in the job you are doing now. For example, you might be the one who can come up with just the right approach to handling problem customers, or you might be the one who shares with the office the idea of putting mirrors on every desk. Mirrors that will reflect the smile that the phone carries across to the customer. You might be able to "read" people effectively and share this information in a meaningful way with your associates. Remember, creativity is finding a way to do something better than it was done, more effectively than thought possible, or just knowing when to use which approaches to enhance productivity.

So generate and apply new ideas every day, make use of old ideas in new ways, and take steps to generate new approaches to the problems you face in dealing with customers. You may enjoy a book by Roger Van Oech called, A KICK IN THE SEAT OF THE PANTS.

CUSTOMER RELATIONS

OLD APPROACH	NEW APPROACH
Deal with problems directly at the desk or counter.	Have customers work with relations to resolve problems.
Train only upper management in appropriate. approaches	Provide training for all staff levels.

Creativity means that you venture off the old roads and open yourself up to new ideas and take advantage of the good ideas all around you. Listen to your customers, identify their problems, and then find new approaches to solve them. It is easy to come up with new ideas, but the hard part is letting go of what worked before. We are really rather timid and scared of change.

"People who are only good with hammers see every problem as a nail." Because we hate to leave "our comfort zone," we are reluctant to explore the unknown because it takes some flexibility, courage, and a willingness to be open to new ideas.

HOW CAN YOU CHANGE?

- Be willing to get out of your comfort zone and try something new.

- Let your child surface. Be curious.

- Know what results you want, and be open to new approaches.

- Brainstorm alone and with others and defer judgment.

- Don't be afraid of new ideas.

- Get out of your rut.

- Explore every idea.

- Look at the big picture, and remember where you have been.

The child is "father of the man," and every adult has a child within that needs to be released. Release your's and learn to look at the world through a child's eyes. See the rainbows in the oil slicks.

KEY STRATEGY #13

STEP OUT OF YOUR BOX.
TAKE A CREATIVE APPROACH
TO YOUR JOB.

14

PACKAGING
MAKES A STATEMENT!!

"The most important facet of any business is
its people, committed management, enthusiastic employees, and customers who are
so satisfied with the service and product,
they tell other people."

Cliff Hiatt
President and CEO
Foster Freeze, International, Inc.

Packaging and dress make a statement that
leaves a lasting impression, and the success
of a product or the success of the interchange are often
directly tied to that initial impact.

DRESS FOR BUSINESS AND YOU
DRESS FOR SUCCESS IN BUSINESS

We judge people by their dress, and so it is no surprise
to learn that they judge us by our's. When we deal

with corporate executives, we expect to find them in conservative business attire, but we are not surprised to find that the film executive appears in a tweed jacket, open throat shirt and slacks. Why? We hold stereotypes of dress that go with different industries, and we want our clients and customers to see us as the person who can handle their business efficiently and effectively.

Your image is also enhanced by good manners and polished behaviors. In fact, one of our associates has built a sizeable business by helping executives and their staffs dress for success and present themselves in the most effective and polished way possible.

The experts tell us that there are a number of elements that go into creating an image remembered with pleasure, and they are

- a genuine interest in others
- a pleasant tone
- a well modulated voice
- sincerity
- concern for others

- a sense of urgency
- a willingness to "go the extra mile"
- a sense of humor
- a pleasant expression (smile)
- good grooming

Not one of these elements costs money, but the end result is often both personal (self confidence and self satisfaction) and monetary gain.

Our business is built upon solving "people problems." Since we found that many questions asked at conferences and conventions deal with the problems people face in developing the right corporate image, we have developed programs to help our clients solve this problem.

SPLIT SECOND EFFICIENCY

Split second efficiency is IMPRESSIVE, and it can be planned. Take a few minutes and look at your own schedule and how it can be tailored to prove to others that you are truly a "pro."

1. Set up phone appointments, and keep them (i.e., if you say that you will call at 8:00 a.m., call promptly at 8:00 a.m.!).

2. If you promise to send out materials on a given day, DO SO. If you say that they will reach someone on a given day, **make sure they do even if Express Mail has to be used!**

3. Look at your desk through a stranger's eyes. Don't make excuses because you are busy. Even non-detail people can be organized. They just may do it in a different way. Try color coding your mail and projects—red for AT ONCE, green folders for RIGHT AWAY, and blue folders for SOMEDAY.

4. Plan ahead, so that you don't waste anyone's time including your own. Keep a time log for a week to see where your time actually is spent, and then analyze it to see how the flow could be improved.

WHAT IMPRESSION DO YOUR LETTERS MAKE?

Every letter or memo you send out is your representative. Is it presenting the image you want others to have of you? Be a stickler about anything that goes out over your name or under your company's logo.

It should be pleasingly formatted, free of errors, neat, with no dabs of "white out." Advertisers have learned that impressions should be positive, and once made are hard to alter. What impressions do your letters or reports make?

Personalize your letters and correspondence. This doesn't have to be a major undertaking with the availability of computers. Even a form letter can have sections held open for personal comments and inserts. In the increasingly impersonal world, the time this takes is minimal compared to the impact it produces.

Express mail, telegrams, and cables carry an aura of importance, but not if you use them over and over again. It is to your advantage to plan ahead and employ these channels only when they will have the most effect.

KEEP YOUR WORD

Although there are times when circumstances beyond your control make it impossible to meet deadlines or deliver products promised. These should be kept to a minimum. When they do occur, the customer has the right to hear why!

However, there are times when it pays to graciously "let people off the hook." They, too, run into situations that make it difficult for them to live up to schedules or commitments or just change their minds. Don't be heavy handed at such times and don't jump in with statements like "But you promised." Give those people a chance to explain and tell you why the change needs to occur. Also, look at it from the vantage point of one year from now–will it matter then? Keep things in proper perspective.

PACKAGING IS IMPORTANT

The advertising industry has taught us a valuable lesson. A person has only 4 minutes to make an impression and a product only 30 seconds. When this is considered, we know why advertising is big-business. The impression YOU make is just as important. What have you done about it?

What is important? Color can be used as a turn on or a turn off. Studies have shown that red is a color which has one of the strongest of all impacts. The retina responds strongly to its stimuli, yet it is not always the appropriate color to use. Customs, traditions, and culture enter into the considerations that need to be given to packaging. Other colors such as pink, white, blue, and green also produce predictable responses, so it is important to consider the impression you want to make and then plan the packaging to produce that impression.

Although graphics, size, color and shape are vital to the success of a product—almost as important as the product itself—there are instances when the quality is so outstanding that the public will overlook the negatives of any of the above and go on buying. For example, consider the number of years Amway went without redesigning the SA8 box (soap), yet a study done two years ago indicated that most of those who had used the soap and were no longer doing so would still use it if they could find a distributor. Other products have made periodic changes, but have continued to keep their basic designs—Morton Salt is one example, and Betty Crocker another (in the latter instance, is was not until 1986 that Betty's hairdo left the 30's).

So if your product is truly unique or the "best" then you may be able to ignore the need for up-to-date packaging. do you want to take the chance?

Coco Chanel once said that if a woman is poorly dressed you notice her dress and if she's impeccably dressed you notice the woman. We believe that if a company cares enough to make certain that their personal and professional "packaging" is of the highest quality, your impressions are positive though you don't analyze why. When they don't take this extra effort, you remember what they did wrong and judge all of their other aspects by the error.

KEY STRATEGY #14

PACKAGE FOR SUCCESS, IMAGE MAKES THE DIFFERENCE.

15

STRESS AND THE CUSTOMER

"The secret of business success is to please the customer–who is always right!!"

Josh Pintel
President
Tom McCall and Associates

One of the major causes of stress is change, and the energy needed to adjust to that change results in a depletion of energy. It is that depletion that results in the stress. If everything were to remain stable and static, little stress would result. Not all stress is bad, for it is our attitude about change that makes the major difference. Those who view potentially stressful situations as challenges, are less negatively affected than are those who see them as problems.

A recent FORTUNE MAGAZINE study of some 500 CEO's (Chief Executive Officers) showed that their mortality rate was actually 37 percent lower than average, and a GALLUP POLL showed that only 19 percent of those running top companies considered stress a problem. However, 23 percent of those running medium-sized companies did, and 49 percent of those running small companies saw stress as a serious factor in their lives. Thus, we can see that the attitude, not the event, causes the stress. Change and the way we respond to it, can generate excitement, serve as a motivator, increase our productivity, and spur us to new heights of achievement.

A nationwide survey recently co-sponsored by Panasonic and Professional Secretaries International found that the biggest stress-inducers were interruptions, lack of advancement opportunities, the inability to share in the decision making process, insufficient communication, low pay, deciding which task to do first, having to take the blame for another's mistake, answering the phone, and having to cope with more than one person at the same time.

Since fifty to seventy percent of all illnesses are stress based, it is important to learn to control that stress, the longer the stress is ignored the more serious the negative consequences. Adrenaline supplies are depleted, blood pressure rises, emotional resilience weakens, and strokes, heart attacks, nervous disorders, and other problems can result.

KEY ISSUES:

All change—personal or job-based—disrupts, creates uncertainty, and reduces productivity. It is vital that you learn to deal with others without buying into their problems and increasing your own stress level. In today's business world, there is more stress than ever before because of the rapidly changing technology and its impact upon the job market and job demands.

The structure of an organization can create stress since a number of factors may be present and contributory. For example,

1. AUTHORITY does not always accompany responsibility.
2. SUPPORT is not always given when needed.
3. EMPLOYEES may not be part of the decision making process.
4. TEAM WORK may not be fostered.
5. Not all COLLEAGUES are teamplayers.
6. ADMINISTRATIVE POLICIES related to work assignments, personal conduct, procedures, and supervisory support may be stressful.

7. There may be no clearcut COMMUNICA-
   TION CHANNELS.

A major problem can result from the gap between
what you expect the job requirements to be and what
the boss expects. A number of our clients have re-
solved this problem by using JOB CHECK to insure
that the position is clearly defined, so that the employee and employer can reach an understanding of
the behaviors which are expected in all aspects of the
position.

Many people are hired after their experience, education, resumes, recommendations, and skills are considered. But people are fired when their behaviors do
not match the expectations which in most cases are
never shared.

IT IS BETTER TO STAY HEALTHY THAN TO TRY TO GET WELL!!

Health is a state of positive mental and physical well-
being. A preventative approach is critical, and it requires that there be regular physical exercise, medical
care, and good nutrition as well as a conscious safety
program.

Since your health affects the way you cope with change and stress, ask yourself the following questions:

1. Do you eat breakfast? If so, what?
2. Do you exercise on a regular basis?
3. What do you do for yourself personally?
4. What type of support system do you have?
5. How can your attitude make a difference?
6. Do you maintain your sense of humor?
7. Do you have a game plan for your life?

Consider your answers carefully, and then make certain that you are taking active and constructive steps to reduce or control the stress and change that is occurring in your life.

Stress reduction experts recommend that all of us use one or more of the following approaches to stress reduction:

1. **IMAGING** requires that you relax and picture a scene that to you is serene and calming. Go there in your mind and see it in vivid detail. Tensions seem to ebb away.

2. **BIOFEEDBACK** is another approach, but it requires specific training in order to be effective.

3. **DEEP BREATHING** is effective for minor situations since it increases oxygen which has a calming effect. In the South Pacific during WWII, oxygen was given to pilots to inhale just before they were sent out on dangerous missions.

4. **EXERCISE** is an excellent approach, and vigorous exercise releases a chemical in the brain which produces a form of euphoria.

Stress, out of control, leads to burnout, so it is necessary to recognize the clues to both in order to stay healthy. There are definite stages to burnout—ongoing fatigue; decreased sociability, a reluctance to get up in the morning, a disinterest in work, decreased productivity, emotional problems, and finally negative physical impact.

Those who feel a sense of purpose and commitment, those who view change as a challenge and not a threat, and those who understand the need to interact effectively aren't affected by stress in a negative way. According to Suzanne Kobasa, a stress researcher, such individuals use stress to sharpen their endurance and coping skills.

KEY STRATEGY #15

**RETURN STRESS TO ITS
RIGHTFUL OWNER.**

<u>YOU</u> TAKE CONTROL.

16

CUSTOMERS: TODAY AND YESTERDAY

"The customer is the guy that makes everything possible!!"

Jerry Breitbart
Senior Advisor
Restaurant Association

"This is the best of all possible worlds and the worst of all possible worlds"–depending upon the person. The work force is spoiled–wants more money; is lazy–wants shorter hours; isn't dedicated–won't stay late; isn't responsible–shops around for a better deal; is slow to pay–depends on credit cards; is hard to deal with–wants attention and lots of questions answered.

Can you relate to the scenario above? It is happening all over America. Communication has broken down, and the results are conflicts and misunderstandings. Part of the problem is due to the fact that 70% of the population is reluctant to embrace–or even accept–change, and yet the world we live and work in now would not be recognized by our grandparents.

How does this affect customer relations? In almost every way.

Customers today are indeed different from those of yesteryear, and we have some major adjustments to make if we are to deal successfully with them. They are better educated (fifty years ago the average Americans didn't even have a high school education, but their grandchildren are often college graduates). Television and improved communication has provided the average American with reservoirs of knowledge previously unknown; thus, those of us in business face a much more sophisticated buying public often trained in the aspects of consumer education. That means that we need to recognize this and know what they have been taught.

The American real estate market profits greatly from the increased mobility of the population—it is estimated that most people move every five years and are upwardly mobile. This mobility has had a major impact upon the customer base since those whose grandparents lived in the same place for years and years and shopped at the same stores for a lifetime, now move about the country and seek new vendors of products and professional services. Whereas, we once were able to get to know our customers and their families, this is now a luxury not available to most of us, and we must now learn to "read" our customers/clients from external clues and deal accordingly with them.

The divorce rate is also impacting upon business in that many women lose a major portion of their spendable income. Thus vendors and professionals whom they previously used either no longer get their business or find that payment plans need to be worked out.

This fact, plus the increased willingness to incur debt, has caused many businesses to have to pull back from offering credit since poor payment patterns often drain resources. In fact, the lack of cash flow has actually sent many businesses into bankruptcy in the past few years. These factors have caused some important changes to occur. Credit checks are more common, and companies are more cautious about those to whom they give credit. Customer relations may suffer from this, so extra care needs to be taken to insure that they protect themselves but not at the loss of customer good will.

In addition to the monetary changes which occur because of divorces, staffs need to be aware that the increased number of single parents, and the increased number of fathers now responsible in part, or all of the time, for raising children have changed buying patterns. This change influences advertising, store layout, store hours, and buying patterns. Many individuals have less time to shop, may need more help in making selections, and may even be vying with the ex-partner in a version of a Power Game.

The changing role of women has to be dealt with also since they are now more assertive, whereas at one time they were the responsibility of the husband. As late as 1971, one of the authors was asked to produce written permission from her husband when she tried to rent a car at O'Hare in Chicago. It was only after she threatened a class action suit, that the car was provided.

Women now have a legal right to their own credit. Those in customer service need to realize, however, that many of those women still have not exercised their rights, and may need help in setting up accounts and learning the process involved in establishing and maintaining a good credit rating.

Rapid changes in the technological world mean rapid changes in the job market. Positions that seem secure disappear with all of the financially negative impact that would be expected. Engineers were laid off by the thousands in the 60's, and the supposedly stable Silicon Valley in California has experienced mass upheavals in the computer industry. Job security is no longer a given fact even in such once stable areas as education, so purchases are often made more cautiously and less impulsively. Major purchases are put off during such downswings, or when interest rates are forced upward. More patience is needed and a more service-oriented customer relations program is demanded by these factors.

White collar crime, shoplifting, and drugs are problems that we face which our grandparents did not have to consider. Internal crime—thefts—erode company profits. These are further reduced by shoplifting which is such a problem that urban-based retail companies factor it into their annual costs.

Drug problems impact in two ways—employees whose productivity is reduced and customers who are erratic—or dishonest—because of the ingestion of such substances. These problems impact upon customer relations programs since there is a need to be wary without conveying suspicion.

With the shift from a farming society to an urban one, the tensions and conditions inherent in crowding, noise, and alienation have fostered behaviors seldom encountered in the past. This means that those involved in customer relations need to compensate for these tensions by increased courtesy, concern, and understanding.

Taxation has made a major difference, too. Prior to the income tax bite, people kept what they earned. Now—even under the new tax laws—major portions of each individual's income are not available to spend. Of course, this affects spending patterns. Many companies are now using very creative approaches to counter this fact–arranging payment patterns accordingly, putting off initial payments until returns come in, or suggesting ways that certain purchases can be considered as business expenses.

What can we learn form all of this? CHANGE is a constant with which we have to deal, and for which we have to adapt our practices as well as our services and products if we are to succeed.

KEY STRATEGY #16

**CHANGE IS A CONSTANT
WITH WHICH WE HAVE TO LIVE AND
TO WHICH WE HAVE TO ADJUST!**

17

MANAGEMENT MAKES A DIFFERENCE IN CUSTOMER RELATIONS

"Tomorrow's retail leaders will be those companies that provide outstanding customer service today, and innovate based on their customer's input in order to remain the industry leader."

Tom Nielsen
Vice President Human Resources
and Customer Service
K MART Corporation

Effective planning is the foundation for on-going success. Effective managers understand those they manage because they can understand their needs and styles. The person who can follow and learn from the leader, is the one who moves rapidly into a position in management.

We have found that the same manager who recognizes the importance of the customer is the one whose staff also puts the customer first. This manager takes a firm stand on the importance of meeting the customers' needs since he realizes that the "customer definitely is king/queen."

A division is only as strong as its management, yet the power of the supervisor lies in his staff. This person also broadens his base by insuring that all of those around him are trained, knowledgeable, and supported. If you staff has to work around you, you became an obstacle, not a support system.

Consider your own management style. Do you

- Give support when it is needed?
- Exercise self-control?
- Try to be fair?
- Strive to be decisive?
- Do more than you get paid for?
- Earn respect?
- Try to be empathetic?
- Assume full responsibility; don't pass the buck?
- Cooperate?
- Have a game plan?

There are several forms of leadership. One group rules by intimidation and the other by consent. People follow the tyrant or dictator for only a limited period of time, but they will follow the other for indefinite periods of time.

It is as important to know what NOT to do as it is to know and use the ten items given. Those who do not last in managerial roles usually cannot organize, aren't creative, and are often selfish and volatile as well as disloyal. Instead of encouraging the staff, fear is used to extract performance. In addition, this leader wants to be judged and paid for what is known, not what is done, and competition is feared.

Those who succeed remember that the public is their partner. Courtesy and service are the key words in today's market place, and when this is forgotten, the person who forgets will lose the privilege to serve. Before the phone company learned the importance of customer relations, we did not hear comments such as "Thank you for using AT&T." What we need to remember is that your conduct shapes your destiny.

Each person is his/her own salesperson for the personal services provided to the customer or client base with which he or she works. The quality and quantity of service given and the way in which it is given determines the results. When managers remember this and train their staff to remember it, too, customer relations are excellent.

Andrew Carnegie stressed the importance of harmony in the workplace, and he said that he would not retain any man who did not work in the spirit of harmony, no matter how great the quantity produced nor how efficient the person. Service should be rendered in a pleasing way, and whether you sell you services or a product, you are no less a merchant, and the buyers are no less clients or customers.

SUCCESSFUL MANAGERS keep their sense of humor, master communication skills, and are flexible and creative when faced with change. An article in the *WALL STREET JOURNAL* indicated that there are well established routes up the corporate ladder. The three most important personal traits needed for advancement were simple virtues: integrity, industriousness, and the ability to get along with people. It was said that employees wishing to move up should demonstrate personal ambition and a commitment to the company and its goals. All other factors (i.e., performance, peer acceptance, problem analysis, pressure handling, politics, and presentation of self), were considered secondary to those noted. Those who move up the corporate ladder do so because they have within them the strength of purpose and the sense of direction needed to pave the way.

KEY STRATEGY #17

MANAGEMENT SETS THE TONE: STAFF IMPLEMENTS IT!

18

THE RIGHT STAFF MAKES THE DIFFERENCE

"Few people in business deal directly with customers, yet they depend on the rest of the organization, that fragile chain, to get products or services to the marketplace. We often forget that directly, or indirectly, we all serve the customer and collectively we win or lose."

Joseph Sakach

Q It costs money to be wrong, and it pays dividends when you are right. As you know, turnover is expensive, and yet most employers have three areas that play an important role in their selection of either full or part-time employees—EDUCATION since it relates to job needs; EXPERIENCE since it may indicate success in similar roles; and PERSONAL PROJECTION which indicates how the person may come across to the customers and clients. Yet, most dismissals are the result of behaviors that don't match expectations. Doesn't that seem a bit illogical. Shouldn't behaviors be factored in, in the first place?

How can that be done? First, do you even know what you really want done? Have you sat down and done a thorough analysis of the responsibilities? How much detail work is going to be required? Must the person make unpopular decisions or handle difficult people? Is persistence to plug away at boring work important? Is caution needed?

If you haven't really determined that above and considered the behaviors you want—pace level, drive level, interactive skills, and rule compliance, how can you expect to find a match to the unknown?

It is imperative that you know what you need before you even begin seeking someone to do the job. Otherwise, you will probably find the person does not do what you "feel" is needed, and the results are bad for you, the successful completion of the workload, the clients and customers, and the ego of the person you hire. Don't expect the employee to "know" what is in your mind—but YOU have to know.

Second, after you have defined the job, you still have to find the employee who can best perform in the position. How do you do that? Obviously, time-tested information you have always used is important–you do need to know what kind of preparation the individual has had, and how well he/she relates to the public.

But there are other important items that successful personnel directors throughout the country have been using for 28 years–items you can also use (If any readers are interested in this list, please fill out the form at the back of the book, and the information will be forwarded).

PREDICTING BEHAVIORS

BEHAVIORS are the key ingredients in any successful job performance, and our behaviors are directed by our values and controlled by our intelligence. It is, therefore, obvious that as employers you need to have a way to find out what that behavior is going to be. There are instruments available that will allow you to graph a job, have an employee do the same, and then compare and contrast the two views.

Equally important is the fact that there are also instruments that will make it possible to learn how the person's behavior is viewed by the public—the source of your business; how the person wishes to be seen by the world; and how the person will behave under pressure or stress. (Information on the instruments designed by our company and used with our clients can also be secured by using the tear out sheet in the back of the book).

There are six basic behavior classics—styles that appear over and over again in the general population, and knowing these styles and what can be expected from each gives you the employer, insight into placement, motivational needs, and possible areas that will be noted or considered under situations which produce stress or pressure.

Many companies—Fortune 500 to small businesses—are using these instruments to help them reduce turnover and increase the chance of selecting the best employee from among the candidates. If you consider the fact that it now costs some $35,000 to replace one mid-level manager and between $50,000 and $100,000 to replace top management, then it is well worth the time and effort expended to insure that the right choice is made in the first place.

If you don't have these instruments at your fingertips, some important information can be derived through observation. For example, if you interview a person who has chosen to wear the "corporate dress" to the interview—dark suit, white shirt, dark tie with a touch of red—and who speaks rapidly, notes on his resume that he belongs to many professional and business organizations, and seems to have chaired many of the committees upon which he has served, then you have a person who in all likelihood has high drive.

Such a person is generally ambitious, likes to take charge, wants to have the "big picture" rather than all of the details, socializes when there is a business "pay off," and is generally happiest in either a sales or a managerial role. Most of the time such people are good at relating to others and work either through them or by directing them.

Now, if the job you have in mind is going to require this person to sit for long hours in relative isolation, you may want to either reshape the job to provide for some of this individual's needs, take a long look at other factors being considered to make certain that the solitude has worked out well in the past, or—if this person is definitely the best candidate—consider the promotional options that will become available and make it possible for him/her to move on into a job that may be more suited to his/her behavior patterns at a point in the future.

Let's be realistic. Many of us hire our "clones," and don't consider other factors. In fact, some of the best business people plan otherwise but end up hiring from an emotional—not a logical—base. Two of our clients interviewed many people trying to find a "detail person" because they were trying to hire to their own weaknesses—they tend to look at the big picture and do not want to be bothered with the details needed to insure its success. Despite this, they allowed themselves to be swayed by the applicant's manner and personality. Because the applicant was very much like them in behavioral style, they decided that she would fit in well with the staff. They learned very soon that she did fit in well, but she too was not a detail person. Now there are three just alike, and the gap still exists.

It is imperative that employers take time to evaluate the job, the employee (there are thirteen factors that are often used as a part of the weighted scale in the evaluation process), and the work environment if they wish to make the personnel process more cost effective. It behooves us to consider every facet of the "hiring fit." Success is dependent upon it.

You have to be able to deliver to YOUR clients and customers and do it more effectively than your competitor, and you have to be able to do it with the best staff possible—a stable one, too. You can not afford to NOT take the time needed to plan. Business problems cripple, and most business problems are really people-based. Take the time to solve your people problems before they happen—at the time you interview, hire, place or transfer an employee.

Remember, we tend to hire by experience, skills, personal projection, and recommendations, but we fire for behaviors!

KEY STRATEGY #18

THE RIGHT STAFF CHOICES CAN MAKE THE DIFFERENCE IN CUSTOMER RELATIONS.

19

TIPS FROM THE FRONT LINE

*Organizations that welcome change and
accept realities find themselves gaining
the competitive edge.*

The most important person in any company is the person who just spoke to, interacted with, or served a client or customer. Since that is the case, it seemed logical to go to those individuals and ask them to share their expertise. We asked them what they believed to be some of the outstanding approaches their companies were currently using to ensure that customers were given the best service possible in the most positive way imagineable, and this chapter shares our findings. But, it goes beyond that, for after doing our interviews, we reviewed the findings (we had divided the responses by the type of organization— entrepreneurial, non-profit, corporate) and learned that there were literally no justifable differences in the strategies used. It really did not matter what size the company (in those areas where advanced technology was not required), what organizational pattern, nor its focus (productivity or profit and productivity), the bottom line was the same. Customers can be served efficiently, effectively,courteously.

PHONES CAN BE AN EFFECTIVE P.R. TOOL

THE 45 MINUTE RULE

Employees from all three types of organizations noted that they followed the "45 minute rule." In other words, it was company policy to return calls within 45 minutes, even when the call involved a negative response.

We then did a survey and found that many companies said they had such a policy, but we found that they did not practice it. The negative impact indicated that customer support would increase markedly if they, too, followed the 45 minute rule.

FOLLOW UP AND SHOW YOU CARE

All three groups indicated that they felt that it was essential that follow-up occur. Many noted that they made an effort to follow up immediately and then later to insure that the "fix" was still working.

Those polled indicated that they are far more loyal to companies where the employees do follow-up, and they are shocked, but delighted—when there is a second follow-up to check on the service or product. The best advertisements in the world can't compete with the good will generated by such employee practices.

LOGGING AND TRACKING

Many of the large organizations, some of the entrepreneurial ones, and almost none of the non-profit agencies indicated that they logged and tracked customer comments and complaints. Those who did indicated that it was one of the most effective practices they used.

Every call should be logged, and the log should indicate

- the purpose of the call
- the caller's name, phone number, and address if possible.

- the solution sought
- the action taken
- the date of the call and the date of the action
- the tracking done to find out the cause of the problem (this may be a multiple stepped process and require research to find out the true cause (it might lead to a vendor whose products are inferior and thus render your's inferior).
- the steps taken to correct the problem
- the date when another call was placed to the customer/client to thank them and let them know what was done.

TELL US HOW WE'RE DOING

It was interesting to note that comment cards were used primarily by large organizations and companies. A few of the smaller ones used them, and not one of the public agencies surveyed did. Those using them indicated that it was not enough to ask customers to fill out comment cards. Someone had to get back to them and thank them for the positive comments and discuss ways to remedy the negatives. One company president makes this his task. It is a large company and could have been delegated, but he felt that the feedback made him far more alert to needed changes, innovations, competition, and thus more responsive.

Because so few people receive such responses, many of those surveyed indicated that they seldom, if ever, filled out such requests. Thus, the companies that put them out are more likely to hear from the extreme reactors and not get a broad based opinion sampling. Using such response cards is valuable, but only if you also respond. Remember we only take the extra step when there is a benefit in it for us—actual or pyschological.

THE RING THAT ALIENATES

There was no consistent policy about transferring calls when taking a break or leaving the area. In many instances large organizations had a policy—not always followed—but many entrepreneurial groups indicated that they did not have the necessary equipment capabilities to do so.

There is no excuse for a ringing, unanswered phone. When a customer or client calls in, they deserve an answer. It is not always possible to be at the desk, but it is possible to make alternative arrangements if you are not.

- transfer the phone to a colleague
- roll the call over to a message center
- attach an answering machine and use it.

Nothing alientates a client faster than being ignored—and a ringing phone that goes unanswered is the ultimate example of being ignored.

THE MODERN ROUND TABLE

Camelot's knights gathered around King Arthur at the round table and discussed plans, early Americans gathered around the round oak table and shared news and problems, and one large organization has initiated a Customer Round Table (other companies have used similar approaches) which meets monthly at a company hosted dinner. The customers/clients and company representatives form a working team to insure that the company meets customer needs, plans for future customer needs, and provides responsive service in all departments. The system works very well.

There are a number of companies that have instituted similar systems. One large school district has monthly coffees with the superintendent and his executive staff. These are held in different parts of the community, so that all of the school district's patrons are able to have questions answered, give input, and make suggestions. A small restaurant in Monterey has an owner who strolls through his restaurant each evening talking to patrons, asking questions, and listening to

suggestions. A world-famous dairy in Connecticut—Stew Leonard's—takes "the pulse of the customers" all day long, and the comment cards are read eight times per day. These comments plus the comments gathered from the personal contact of the owner, his staff, and family are all factored into their decision making process.

A TWENTY FOUR HOUR HOT LINE THAT COOLS DOWN CUSTOMERS

A number of large organizations have 24 hour hot lines that take orders, provide data, and give product updates, and many non-profit organizations had similar services. This service has become more common over the past few years, but it is still not common in small companies.

There is no reason why that answering tape couldn't provide some information on a 24 hour basis though. It would mean that someone had to update it daily, but think of the customers who would be able to call in after hours and alleviate some of the pressure on work hours employees.

SERVE CUSTOMERS BY NETWORKING AND NETWORKING UNDER THE NETWORK

Although there was no consistent policy noted, a number of employees noted that they made a practice of learning as much about corollary services as they could. Companies and organizations that also interfaced with their customer base were researched, so that they could make suggestions and give referrals when their customers needed something that they did not or could not provide. It was their contention that customers should be served as one would serve a friend—as broadly as possible.

This concept has real merit. For example, if a consultant is unable to provide the type of program that a client needs, it would be very beneficial to the client if that consultant had the contacts to help track down another who could provide the service. It would help the client in two ways— provide the service needed and provide the service by someone who was not picked at random from the phone pages. Thus, there is a greater likelihood that the quality would come closer to what is wanted than might happen by random chance.

LISTEN, WRITE IT DOWN, AND KEEP THE NOTES

All three groups—entrepreneurial, organizational, and non-profit—noted the importance of taking down what is heard, repeating it back, and then keeping the notes for future reference. A system needs to be in place to make certain that this happens.

One more step needs to be taken. Information that impacts on others needs to be shared and a way devised to work as a team to help the client.

PUT THE POWER WHERE THE ACTION IS—ON THE FRONT LINE

Those who were most proud of their companies indicated that they were given the respect and trust that their positions warranted. They were told to make decisions, within the boundaries of company policy, of course. In addition, they were backed up by their companies when they did.

Some delightful stores were shared. One young man worked for a large power company, and he told about an employee who was charged with keeping the power up and running no matter what

the weather conditions. During the bitter storms of 1989, power lines went down on a mountaintop in the NorthEast. There was no transportation into the area—roads were shut down, phone lines were down, and power was off. He made a decision. He rented a helicopter, flew to the remote area with a crew, repaired the lines, and flew back. Power was restored, and the company continued to meets its client obligations. What happened to him? He was praised for his concern and problem solving. True, this is an extreme situation, but companies should consider the fact that they hire adults—if they don't that means that they have need to revamp their hiring policies—and they need to be trained to think, problem solve, and act in the best interest of the client and the company.

KNOWLEDGE—A POWERFUL CUSTOMER SERVICE BASE

All of those polled indicated that they believed it essential for every person to be well informed about company policy, the company mission, as well as new products and services. In other words, they saw a need for an on-going information system to be in operation.

There are many ways to insure that such a system exists. For those with computers, it is easy to put messages and informational updates on the screen. For those based in widely divergent areas, there are voice mail systems that make it possible to put multiple messages in all at one time—time is energy and money, so the ease of one message and multiple receivers should be welcome to employee and employer alike. Memos are also effective if kept short and limited to one topic.

During the interviews and discussions, many interesting and very viable approaches were mentioned, and although they were not widely used, they seemed like excellent ideas to share. Consider a **newsletter** which will share information with both internal and external customers. There could be two, there could be one with an insert for the internal customers (colleagues), or there could be just one serving both. Whatever, it keeps everyone up-to-date, and information is an effective public relations tool.

One-on-one meetings are also effective, and bonding and rapport build rapidly in such situations. Also, a **customer service ombudsman or advocate** takes the pressure off many staff members and also insures that customer problems are dealt with in an efficient and timely manner.

Internal monitoring has paid dividends in effective telephone service in one company wherein the President makes a practice of dialing internal numbers at random for 10 minutes each day. He listens to the tone, manner, and message and then makes either pleasantly worded constructive comments or gives the employee a compliment for the effective and pleasant manner in which he/she answered the telephone.

It's not an interruption, its an opportunity. At least that is what one small company has had affixed to each telephone. Thus, employees are reminded that no matter how busy they are, that caller is not an interruption, but the one for whom the whole organization runs.

The size of the company, the product sold, the service rendered—none of these changes the necessity for providing the quality of customer service that distinguishes the best from the "also rans" in business. Only by taking time to understand customers, identify their needs, recognize their priorities, and serve them can a company hope to maximize its own potential.

We would like to thank the employees in the following industries who were kind enough to share with us the things that made their organizations and companies worth noting as positive contributors to customer service.

Ambrosia Chocolate
Bald Precision Parts
Best Foods
Bloomberg Financial Markets
Daily Record Newspaper
Delta
Direct Mail Services
Firemaster
G.E. Capital
H. & M. International
Meadowlands Hospital
N.J. Transit Corporation
Office Business Systems
Paper Plus Company
Prudential Insurance Company
Ridgewood Water Department
Six Flag Great Adventure
Syntrex
Teledyne
Yugo American

CUSTOMER SERVICE EVALUATION

Read through the items below and check those that you do. This will help you evaluate your own customer service program.

_____ 1. All phone calls are logged and tracked.

_____ 2. All calls are returned promptly.

_____ 3. All questions are followed up and the customer is told the action being taken.

_____ 4. Each customer is given personalized service.

_____ 5. Each employee is given recognition for accomplishments — an on-going process.

_____ 6. CSR personnel are given authority to act along with the responsibility to do so.

_____ 7. The customers "pulse" is taken often, and the findings incorporated into planning.

_____ 8. Attention is given to details—employee dress, condition of the store, length of lines, phone answering response time, etc.

____ 9. An employee incentive program is in place.

____ 10. The attractiveness (i.e., condition, cleanliness, etc.) of the facility is maintained and stressed.

____ 11. The quality of the materials sent out is monitored and maintained.

____ 12. Staff input and ideas are encouraged and rewarded.

____ 13. Customer responses are sought (i.e. comment cards), noted, and follow-up correspondence sent to the customer. In addition, action is taken promptly.

____ 14. Phones are always covered and answered within 4 rings.

____ 15. Teamwork is taught and encouraged.

____ 16. Management is committed to the concept of quality customer service.

____ 17. Future customer needs are analyzed and plans devised to meet them.

____ 18. Competitor's services are analyzed and used as a yardstick for self-assessment.

____ 19. Satisfaction is guaranteed.

____ 20. Change for improvement is encouraged.

20

MODELING FOR
SUCCESS

"The essence of customer service is simple. Treat the customer with respect, give him more than he expects, and make the experience of dealing with your company as easy as possible."

Paul B. Brown
"For Service Please Hold," Inc.
May 1898

'C lass," "Innovation," "Strategist" all three terms can be used to describe those who succeed and then keep their market share in this highly competitive world. The people we are about to introduce can be described as "class acts," whose 'innovative" approaches, and well planned "strategies" have put them in the forefront of their industries. In each case, they kept in mind the key to success—the customer's satisfaction, and it is their strategies that we would like to share with you in this chapter.

FROM CATALOGUES TO RETAILING: THE J. CREW WAY

Although Arthur Cinader, J. Crew's Chairman, has been involved in the catalog business for quite some time, J. Crew itself was started only six years ago by him. His daughter, Emily, has provided input and direction that has been a critical factor in the company's success and has helped it achieve the stature that it enjoys today. She analyzed the market she wanted and then used the catalogue images to target that audience. Not for her the trout stream, but instead co-educational, lively, fast track activities and models.

Her views exemplify the value she and her company place upon quality and simplicity of design coupled with practicality. She recently found an old anorak hanging in a closet at the family cabin. Its age? Well, her father was wearing it when he first met her mother, but there it was. As she noted, "it...weathered pretty well." As was noted in SAVVY, she wants "everything she makes to work as well as that old anorak."

This attitude is part of the reason that J. Crew is moving into an increasingly powerful position in the marketplace. Another, and a major reason, is the dream they sell. Successful salesmen have made millions by helping people dream and then claim that dream, and J. Crew is duplicating this highly success-ful process through its packaged dreams—dreams with which common people can identify (bike trips through the Northeast, weekends in Hawaii). There is a subliminal message in each catalogue. That girl in hot pink stepping out of the surf is not only selling a tank dress, she is selling a lifestyle. The duality of the message demands that there be careful scrutiny of all details, and Ms. Cinader excels in this.

In order to meet the needs of the market she has targeted, Ms. Cinader and her father plan, supervise, orchestrate, and practice what is the key to all good management—the team approach to hands-on super-vision. One of the keys to effective customer service is to have someone dedicated at the top. The attitude of the top personnel will be the attitude of those on the front line. No amount of talk covers up the fact when the words are not supported by action. In order to succeed, it is necessary to walk what you talk, and in this case we might want to change that verb to run. For, J. Crew literally runs forward to meet its cus-tomers.

When asked to share some specifics related to their operation, management, and customer service ap-proaches, the staff at J. Crew, Inc. was very helpful and the Director of Publicity, Jennifer Riegel, gathered the requested data which we have set forth below:

J. Crew gets input from their customers in a variety of ways. Every operator is equipped with a stack of "customer feedback forms," and these are filled out by the operator who takes the call. Thus, it is possible to determine patterns in complaints or praises. In addition to being reviewed and analyzed, each month these comments—negative and positive—are forwarded directly to the President for review and consideration.

All companies encounter concerned customers, and the staff at J. Crew takes time to "listen" to their patrons, no matter how angry they may be. They take great care to interact with them calmly and accord them respect. In addition, each person's concerns are given serious consideration, made known to top management, and changes in policy have resulted from comments delivered in person or by letter.

Not satisfied with waiting for comments, J. Crew also conducts surveys and focus groups to learn more about reactions to policies or merchandise and to identify any specific problems that may be of concern.

Obviously, management has played a key role in setting this policy for truly listening and responding to customers just as management plays a key role in the entire customer service program. Every customer's letter is read personally by a member of management, and many have been known to pick up the telephone and personally call the concerned party.

The key to the success of this rapidly expanding company can be summed in up three words—**concern for customers.**

This concern translates into action based upon direct interaction and response. Who wins—the company and the patrons.

CATALOGUES ARE
BIG BUSINESS

Folksy and modern sounds like an unlikely combination, but it isn't when you are referring to L.L. Bean. This corporation set in Portland, Maine, has a long standing courtship underway—a courtship with customers from the wilds of Wyoming to the concrete towers of New York and Los Angeles.

Most of us think of a catalogue when we hear the name L.L. Bean—60 million catalogues to be exact, but there is far more to this company which minds the store 24 hours a day. Running a 50,000 square foot store which never shuts its doors and has racked up 253.7 million dollars in store and catalogue sales in one year (1984) sounds like a task for the most sophisticated of modern technology, and it is. But over 7,000 companies have tried to tap this market, and the average catalogue shopper hears from Sears, Penney's, Spiegel, Saks Fifth Avenue, American Express, Lillian Vernon, Lands' End plus hundreds of others.

From its early catalogues in which L.L. Bean admonished his customers not to throw away used Maine Hunting Shoes ("Its about the same as throwing away a $5 bill)," the company has worked to provide a personal relationship with its buyers. The fact that they are known for their no-nonsense business philosophy of selling good merchandise at reasonable profits, and treating their customers like human beings, so that they will always come back for more.

Behind the old-fashioned approach is a computer driven organization which delivers millions of orders annually with a 99 percent level of accuracy (*U.S. News and World Report, March 25, 1985*). When the phone rings it is answered by one of several hundred operators which have been divided into teams of 20. Each team is supported by from 2 to 4 (depending upon the season) team leaders, and during the Christmas holidays the staff is doubled in order to accommodate the customers and make certain that they are not kept waiting.

The team concept is a cornerstone of the company philosophy; the team training and team assignments, seem to have paid off in real teamwork and bonding. Many of the team members enjoy outside activities together, too, and friendships begin and grow in the cooperative atmosphere which is encouraged within the organization. The monthly team meetings are standard, but additional meetings are held when new products are introduced, and additional news is shared through the team newsletter.

The customer service motto is still in place at this giant of the industry, and one of the reasons that people can deliver the kind of service they do is the extensive, in-depth training. Each employee is given 40 hours of training before he or she ever gets on the phone. These sessions are conducted for groups of between 20 and 25, and participants are given an opportunity to role play, taught the basics of courtesy, and the specifics of their responsibilities and obligations to customers.

One of the tips given is to let angry customers vent, and the professionalism of the staff is attested to by the fact that the customer service department is given a great deal of latitude as to what they can and can not do.

Phone service quality is monitored every two to three weeks, conversations are listened to, and input is given as to ways interaction could be improved. What could be a threat is not because the information is shared in a positive, supportive way.

In order to determine current customer needs, input from buyers is sought, and this information is factored into the planning strategies. Staff is encouraged to remember that people are the customers, and a bulletin board shares customer letters and comments.

Of great importance to employees is the fact that there is a real opportunity for personal and professional growth and some excellent "perks". For example, there is a store at which only employees can shop, and the discounts are VERY generous, and employees are also encouraged to borrow items and then provide feedback on them to management. Thus, not only are customers solicited for input, so are staff members.

Customers tend to think of the phone when they think of the company, but teamwork goes way beyond these frontline people. The success of the company and the satisfaction of the customers is due to a true team— order takers, order processors, packers, shippers, and management. It is this cooperative approach that has led the company to work hard to reduce turnaround time without losing quality control.

The changing consumer market has been analyzed, and although many of the old stand-bys are still available, new items are being added all the time. In fact, this willingness to change and fit the new demands is not always in keeping with the desires of some of the old customers who may not handle change as well as this company founded almost eight decades ago.

Even though the company studies market changes and adjusts to meet new needs, one adjustment it has not made is in its return policy—a no questions asked, 100% return policy is, and always has been in effect ever since those first boots that fell apart, were returned, and prompted Bean to return to the "drawing board" to build a boot that worked so well it founded one of the country's customer service dynasty's

ONE COMPANY FOLLOWS
THE PLATINUM RULE

Another retail chain (60 stores) which is fabled for its extraordinary customer service is Nordstrom, a Seattle based company whose sales associates operate almost as entrepreneurs. Management has a guide sheet that they give to all new hires which tells them to use their good judgment in all situations. They note that each person should have personal and professional goals and ask questions at any time. This simple guide sheet has resulted in a store chain which customers believe is wonderful.

The Nordstrom family introduced the concept of commission selling. In this chain, successful employees are both entrepreneurial and intensely loyal to the company, and the majority of their 30,000 employees work well in an environment that encourages them to be team players in "their company." Word has it that there are many of these same employees who pull down incomes between $40,000 and $60,000 per year thanks to the hefty commissions.

Obviously, in order to make this kind of money in an industry which is not noted for high salaries, it is necessary for the employee to do what most successful salespeople in other fields do—meet customer needs, encourage return business, go the extra mile, and do it all in a professional and upbeat way. True, this type of service is not something today's average retail store employee is used to giving, but it pays dividends to those who are willing to accept the pressure and realize that base pay plus hefty commissions demands energy, dedication, and time (sometimes—time beyond the normal 9-5 hours).

In order to reward effort—not TOJ (time on job), Nordstrom developed a system called SPH (sales per hour ratio). The actual SPH (sales minus merchandise returned by customers, divided by hours worked) for each two week period is calculated and appears on each paycheck stub. If the salesperson exceeds the target SPH (which is determined by departmental assignment and hourly wage, the employee is paid a commission ranging from 6.75% to 10.0 % (the figure depends upon the departmental assignment). If the SPH drops below the target, the employee is paid the base hourly wage. One employee indicated that she received $9.00 per hour. Evaluations include an analysis of the overall SPH pattern, and future assignments are in part dictated by the overall picture according to the **Los Angeles Times** article which appeared on 2/4/90.

Although employee reaction to this incentive program is generally positive, some would prefer less pressure. The monetary edge that goes to those who "go the extra mile" is considerable, and although no manager ever tells an employee that he or she may find it necessary to put in hours beyond hourly paid time, some choose to do so. In many instances, they send out thank you notes to past and present clients, call customers to alert them to products going on sale or being ordered, drop off purchases at a special customers home if normal delivery doesn't fit in with time needs (in most instances this is on company time , but in some cases, it may be time they choose to use off the clock). In other words, they do what old-fashioned entrepreneurs did without thought—they become the customer's support system.

In order to generate the enthusiasm needed in any successful sales organization, management conducts store meetings geared to result in positive teamwork. It is of interest to note, that there are no sales training meetings conducted in this chain AT ALL. In a recent article in the **Los Angeles Times** **(2/4/90)**, Betsy Sanders, Vice President and General Manager of Nordstrom's Southern California stores (which employ 11,000 people), was quoted as having said, "philosophically and in practice...what we are talking about is the essence of what Nordstrom is and what we do...The company **is** our employees."

Unfortunately, labor law does not factor in entrepreneurial undertakings, and Nordstrom has run up against statutes that demand that time off the clock spent by emloyees—time they chose to spend—must still be paid time. According to Sanders, working for Nordstrom is rather like going to college at Stanford—intense, competitive. A place where your fellow students [employees in this case] are aggressive, self-motivated, "A" students. These students [employees] work way beyond the estimated study hours to achieve the level of excellence they deem important, to secure the "A" grades they want, and to get the emotional rewards success brings to them.

The Nordstrom system for providing top quality customer service and rewarding top performances is outstanding. The suggestions we have made in some-what similar situations to our clients is that they might want to consider the six value-based motivators which are inherent to us all . The dominant motivational patterns differ from person to person, and those who are not monetarily driven may want the money an-other has, but be motivated to action by a markedly different motivator (time with the family, security, authority). It is, therefore, important for employers to consider various motivational packages and fit them to the unique needs of the staff. After all, there are both **internal and external** customers, and each needs to have its needs met.

MOVING FROM FOUR TO FIVE STAR SERVICE

Five Star service is the goal of the Worthington staff, and they are moving rapidly toward that goal. The Worthington Hotel of Fort Worth , Texas, is already a Four Star hotel, and each employee is given a gold, five star pin to wear. This pin reminds them of their goal according to Nancy Scott who took time from her hectic duties to share with pride information on this beautiful hotel which covers two city blocks.

Although it has only been in operation for nine years, it has already established itself as one of the loveliest properties in the Dallas area. Owned by the Bass brothers (investors whose holdings range from oil to a major stock share of Disney), this 500+ room hotel is run by a staff of some 650 employees every one of whom believes in the philosophy that it is essential to listen to the customer and strive to provide the most personalized and supportive service possible.

This fact was attested to by the staff in general and by the General Manager in particular, and it was he, Dustan Goodell, who provided us with the following tips for our readers.

He noted that the role of top management is to **set** the example. He believes that, "management (at all levels) must adhere to the standards they prescribe for their employees. These ranges from "clean as you go," to attendance, professionalism in behavior and dedication to the mission. If top management is focused on upholding the standards of operation, customer service (**outstanding** customer service) is the inevitable result.

In order to make certain that every employee is as dedicated to the principles of quality service as the management is, Mr. Goodell believes that it is necessary to stress and build upon the concepts expressed through four adjectives—practical, detailed, patient, and cross.

Practical training for our industry means that employees need to "experience" training (monitoring incoming reservation calls, observing check-ins, etc.) **Do not train antiseptically.**

Detail your training with goals and objectives **to be** achieved during the training process. Do not develop a "what should we do today?" mentality. A checklist approach to training will keep both the trainer and the trainee focused.

Patience is not only a virtue, but a necessity in training. You are in essence a teacher and each "student" is going to learn at a different pace. Be tolerant and understanding of errors. And, finally, there is nothing more counter-productive than learning only part of something. Cross-training in all related areas is a **must** if you strive for top employees.

He noted that consistently practicing all four steps takes longer than other approaches, but, in his estimation, the results and end product are definitely worth the wait!!

One of the most common concerns expressed by CSR's (customer service representatives) is having to deal with angry customers. Mr. Goodell gives some very sound advice—**listen...listen...and then think about what you listened to!!** He points out that one only fuels the fire by offering either excuses or explanations. Instead, he suggests that you "take immediate steps to resolve the problem or contact someone in authority who can." He believes that when "a problem is handled professionally, compassionately, and in a timely fashion, nine times out of ten...the situation will turn around and **win** a long-term customer."

Of course, to succeed there needs to be teamwork, and that means that you must "strive to generate input from all departments at all levels. Especially in problem solving situations, elicit information from all parties. Nancy Scott (who is actually a charter member of the staff having been there since the hotel opened) expanded upon this point. She indicated that all comments from customers are charted and those charts are hung in each department. Thus, everyone is made aware of concerns, compliments, areas of need and change. She indicated that they were all encouraged to "listen" and "respond." In addition to responding to the customer and his/her needs, they were also encouraged to respond by providing input on potential solutions and changes.

Her comments were elaborated upon by her boss and colleague, Mr. Goodell, who gave specific directions for getting that input. "**Ask**...this sounds silly but few people **really ask.** Call the group contact...make a special trip to their office...shake their hands, and **ASK!!!** I strongly recommend personal contactwith your clientele.

Mr. Goodell espouses a management approach that should be the standard in all industries—"As the top manager, never take full credit for any event ....delegation is not simply for passing out work...**pass out praise!!!**" In other words, set the example, for lip service will always be detected and eventually be the organization's downfall.

Be positive and follow Ken Blanchard's advice, "find your employees doing something right." Anyone can critique or criticize. It is the easiest thing known to man.

A manager who leads by example, sets obtainable goals, and then applauds accomplishment of these goals will not fail. If goals are not met, do not criticize. Find out why and redirect the efforts of your team toward success.

Every tip given by this very successful manager uses a humanistic approach in an industry that is totally "people focused." To others in the same industry, he suggests that "a humanistic approach in a very human industry will help build a strong group of people with one common goal— to provide superior guest service that will distinguish them as one of the best in their business."

A DAIRY STORE THAT LOVES CUSTOMERS

One of the world's most famous food retailers is Stew Leonard who with his wife risked everything they owned in 1969 to start what is now the world's largest dairy store. This sprawling eight-and-one-half acre complex serves over 100,000 customers each week. Just think, that would fill the Rose Bowl every week of the year!!

The Leonard family, for this is still a family operation, has proven that it is possible to build a business from small to large without sacrificing quality of product or service. This unique organization is built on the foundation of teamwork— in fact, over 55% of the staff of 500 also have a relative or family member working in this store. Some of the tips he so willingly shares and practices are the reason that he was awarded the Presidential Award for Entrepreneurial Excellence by President Reagan in 1986 and why Tom Peters, co-author of IN SEARCH OF EXCELLENCE, said "We've searched the world over looking for excellence, in every nook and cranny, and one of the best examples we've found is a dairy store in Norwalk, Ct.—Stew Leonard's."

Stew emphasizes that "best not biggest" is his goal, for it is not how big the company gets but how good it becomes that is the key to its success in serving customers effectively. He went on to say

- good service is basic and simple—so simple that people tend to overlook it. Just remember who the customer is—**you**—and remember that there is "no rope on customers to bring them back. The only way to get them to return is to make them happy."

- that "profit is not your right. It is a reward for doing a good job."

Managers should take note of his approach to effective management. He believes that "like rain, the concern for good customer service must come from above. It can't be delegated, for the top sets the pattern." In other words, the person at the "top is the key and can—has to—make the difference."

Customer service, however, can not be left to chance, and he believes that "controls must be set up to make it work and to make certain that it runs according to plan." This means that it is necessary to

- get feedback—take the pulse of customers daily.

- manage by "walking around."

- remember that delegated problems never get done.

- accept the fact that if the leadership really wants change it will occur.

- listen to the customers, for those who refuse to change will lose their business edge.

To emphasize his point, he shared some very graphic examples of others who believe as he do that "ivory towers close down." He talked about Ray Crock (the founder of MacDonald's) who with his wife went into one of their stores, did not like what he saw, shut and locked the door, and put a sign up saying that it would reopen later. As frustrated customers lined up outside, frustrated staff gathered around inside asking how they were to serve those customers who couldn't get in. He informed them that the doors would stay closed until the standards of operation were met. Amazing changes occurred in a very short time, and the doors were reopened on an operation that was now up to

Crock's standards. Another person who practices what Stew Leonard believes to be the essence of good management is Sam Walton, founder of Walmart, who makes it a practice to travel around the country, dropping in on his stores, listening to customers, observing conditions and behaviors, and demanding that responsibility be taken for running each operation according to the standards of maintenance and customer service that he established for the first store ever opened.

Stew made his last point by sharing a story about an experience of Murray Raphel, a friend of his. It seems that Mr. Raphel and his wife had been hearing an ad run by a local store. The ad said that to those who came through the check out lines they would say, 'Thank you. Have a nice day." If the cashier failed to do so, the customer was to be given $1.00. The idea intrigued the Raphels who later stopped off at one of the stores to shop. After the bill had been rung up, the cashier told them they owed $30.90. They paid, he took the money, made change and handed it back. Mr. Raphel informed him that he was entitled to $1.00 more because the cashier had forgotten to say, "Thank you. Have a nice day." "Oh, no I don't," said the cashier...That was last month's campaign." The point? You need to walk what you talk. Radio claims, advertisements, T.V. promotions are all words. The only reality is action. Customer service has to begin with each employee.

We like that idea, so we decided to find out about customer service as it was delivered in this world-famous store. Our findings are set forth in the list below:

1. All of the suggestions in the suggestion box are read within 48 hours, noted, evaluated, and—if possible— acted upon.

2. A monthly focus group meets with customers and encourages negative feedback which they believe will help them improve.

3. Fresh flowers are placed in rest rooms daily.

4. The 6,000 pound rock outside the store has their policy carved on it.

    > Rule 1—The customer is always right.
    > Rule 2—If the customer is ever wrong, reread Rule 1.

5. There are animated shows throughout the stores, and a high tech state of the art animation is used.

6. T.V. monitors by the registers show happy employees around the store.

7. Business and school tours are provided, and a senior citizens bus picks up seniors three days per week.

8. There are 28 check out registers for faster service.

9. The employee of the month is posted at the entrance.

10. The "bags around the world" program provides customers with a $3.00 gift certificate for bringing in a picture of themselves in front of a famous landmark with a Stew Leonard bag.

11. Employees are given recognition on a Ladder of Success which is displayed in front of the registers.

12. Free ice cream coupons are given to children. Free ice cream cones are given to mothers if their receipt reaches $100.00.

13. Upset customers are given bouquets of flowers.

14. Special orders are filled when called in.

15. When lines get longer than 3 people, cookies are handed out to those in line.

16. Free samples are distributed 7 days a week.

17. When a customer forgets something and is already in line, staff calls the department and has it brought to the check out line.

18 They don't train employees to be nice, they hire nice people to train!!!

19. There are 10 public telephones for customer convenience.

20. When customers have car trouble in the parking lot, the staff goes out and helps.

21. When the customer wants a product that they don't carry, staff calls other stores, finds it if possible, and then directs the customer to that store.

22. Employees receive free lunches on their birthdays.

23. The store is always decorated for every holiday.

24. Lots of different employee incentives to keep the morale up.

As you can see, service to internal (employees) and external customers is the keystone of the success of this world-renowned retailer.

A ROLE MODEL
TO REMEMBER

"The successful companies will be those where the employees have a stake," according to Dr. Gordon E. Forward, the President of Chaparral Steel Company based in Midlothian, Texas. In addition, he believes that everyone should be included in the process known as participatory management, and for this reason he encourages them to participate.

This fact is attested to by one worker who indicated that he can talk to his supervisor or any of the top personnel with equal ease since management encourages that ideas be shared. Since this is the case, people tend to go out of their way to do things a little better, work a little harder, and share a little more. In other words, in his view, "It is a great place to work." Chaparral has managed to build a company that values its employees and practices **effective internal customer service.**

Chaparral's President says there are two primary reasons—technology and people—for the success of his company when competitors were suffering from the downturn in the market. According to an article published in *MUSE AIR MONTHLY*, June 1984, there were 850 employees at the Midlothian plant doing the work it would take 2000 to 5000 employees in other plants to produce. At that time, Japan's average steel employee produced 850 tons per year vs. Chaparral per employee production of 1300. In many cases we would consider the downside of this—undue pressure upon staff, but the comments of those employed by this company paint an entirely different picture.

This same article listed some innovative approaches used by the company—approaches which we believe may well contribute to the employee's high level of satisfaction.

- There are no time clocks in this plant. Everyone is on salary.

- Paperwork is kept to a minimum—in fact, it is almost non-existent.

- There are no reserved parking spaces— everyone, the President included, parks on a first come, first parked basis.
- The personnel department runs lean—only

six people, and foremen do all hiring.

- Promotions are from within the company, and most of the foremen came up through the ranks.

- There are only 4 levels of decision-making (one GM plant had 17).

All of the above seems to build from the recurring theme in this company—one of which is a trust in people and their ability to accomplish great things. When James Campbell Quick and David A. Gray wrote about this company in an article, "Chaparral Steel Company: Bringing 'World Class Manufacturing' to Steel," [*NATIONAL PRODUCTIVITY REVIEW/* Vol. 9, No. 1, Winter 1989/90], they referred to the importance of this factor. "This trust in the responsibility of employees is behaviorally manifested by the absence of time clocks in the workplace. In addition, no one walks off a post until a replacement reports. This sense of trust and personal responsibility begins at the top. The officers have created a psychologically safe work environment through the leadership they exhibited."

Because management believes that people want to grow and develop, they promote and encourage initiative, curiosity, and provide a culture that focuses upon learning as a valued process.   In order to foster learning and professional growth, the company co-sponsored a program with the U.S. Department of Labor's Bureau of Apprenticeship and Train ing. The program blends OJT (on-the-job-training) and class-room instruction and does so in a cross job/cross level approach which introduces participants to the latest in technical training.

Last, but far from least in the line-up of valuable approaches, is the value placed upon humor and humility by top management. When frustration and pressure are off-set by humor, the end result is a climate that is positive and emotionally rewarding to employees, and such is the case at Chaparral where employees find that their jobs are both personally and professionally rewarding. As Tom Peters pointed out in an article printed in the San Jose Mercury News, 12/17/87, this company is a unique "blend of high technology and wide-open organizational style..."

Although their service center plays a key role in their marketing strategy, the real key to the success of this company is its dedication to the concept of exemplary internal "customer service"—the belief in, support of, and encouragement of its employees.

If there is a magic formula for success it is **customer service, and** these companies that have gained world-wide recognition and success have used this formula.

So can you. Just remember, worry about what is best for the customer, and what is best for the company will automatically follow.

KEY STRATEGY #20

CUSTOMER SERVICE: IS THE MAGIC FORMULA FOR SUCCESS IN ANY INDUSTRY

21

SERVICE SUCCESS
MODELS

"Customers are your company's
advisers. Listen to them."

Homer R. Bandley
Past President
Utah Restaurant Assoc.

In our research which took us from coast to coast in the United States, we learned that those who are at the top of the service industries are there because they have factored in the human element—the element that demands a more personalized service than our parents received. These companies have returned to the small town concept so often lauded in movies, books, and plays—the concept that customers are friends to be served with dignity, graciousness, and attentiveness. The companies we have chosen to use as models all exemplify these "virtues."

A CUSTOMER SERVICE TRIP
TO THE MAGIC KINGDOM

Disney's Magic Kingdom is dedicated to creating a happy experience—Disney style—for everyone who enters this "land of dreams." In order to ensure that this occurs, "rehearsals" begin from the moment someone is hired. Disney University conducts orientation programs, uses discussion groups, provides films, slides, and handbooks as training tools, and takes new "cast" members on familiarization tours geared to increasing knowledge and customer service awareness.

Training continues after the employee is an active member of the "University," too. The university staff concerns itself with the development of the employee as a "total" person—both professionally and socially in line with Walt Disney's belief that prompted him to provide continuing educational programs for all of his employees which he believed paid dividends in enhanced customer satisfaction.

The programs are diverse and cover such a wide variety of topics as Food and Merchandising, technical knowledge, effective management, corporate operation. It is the goal of all of these programs to instill in each employee a sense of unity, a sense of belonging, and a sense of dedication to all that makes "Disney Disney."

Walt Disney believed that effective communication was vital "to the survival of a civilized humanity," and the University staff has developed a system of communications that insures that the "internal" customers (employees) are served as well. Employee publications such as weekly newsletters, humorous in-house magazines, and special bulletins help "cast" members keep in touch with each other and the company. In addition, bulletin boards, film presentations, slide shows, and handbooks are coordinated with opinion polls, questionnaires and frequent discussion groups in order to support and provide an effective, efficient internal communication and feedback process.

In an organization as large as Disney's, it is not unusual to find employees feeling "left out of the information circuit." This is avoided at Disney's various locations through a Cast Communication Network, a closed-circuit television system designed to inform them of company-wide events and happenings. Easy viewing is assured by having various congregation centers set up with television monitors which carry this special programming.

Stress is detrimental to productivity and morale, and Walt Disney realized this and set up sports events to help reduce the tensions under which his creative employees worked. Disneyland's Recreation Club (cast activities) provides a relaxing outlet by offering social and recreational activities. For example, employees (cast members) can attend musicals at the Los Angeles Music Center, vacation at Lake Tahoe, take part in annual canoe races, play on the softball team, compete in basketball tourneys, ski, perform in a company choral group, or display their own creative arts and crafts.

Perhaps this concern for others which is manifested in a concern for employees and customers is the primary reason why Disney employees seem to be part of an extended family—a family that plays and works together and strives to achieve and carry on Disney's dreams. Anyone "can dream, create, design, and build ....but it requires people to make that dream a reality." At Disney, the staff continues to believe in this axiom, and this team sees the public as part of the team as well.

Under the direction of Michael Eisner and President Frank Wells, Disney has turned the corner, moved back from the brink of takeover that faced them in 1984, and reanimated a "fantasy factory" that sets the pace for the entertainment industry.

SKY HIGH CUSTOMER SERVICE

From high hopes, a dream, and an ambitious plan, Fred Smith founded **Federal Express** which though under-capitalized managed to capture 19% of the air express market within three years. This is truly an "overnight" success story of a company that has set astounding growth and revenue records in only a few years. From 14 sleek Falcon jets carrying only 186 packages on that first day, Fred Smith's dream company now employs 80,000 quality-focused people who operate a fleet of 331 airplanes, 30,000 trucks and vans, and processes 6 million packages a week.

Obviously any company growing this rapidly will have some growing pains, but a story that circulates among staff explains why nothing has daunted the founder or his service oriented staff. Managers are encouraged to remember that if a bear and an alligator were to have a fight, the outcome would be determined by the location of the fight rather than the power and skill of the adversaries. According to Bill Razzouk, Vice President of U.S. Sales, the edge does not go to the person quoting numbers, but to the one who creates a satisfied customer when the transaction is ended. "We need to understand the customer's business first, speak his language, and learn about his needs, goals and objectives." (PERSONAL SELLING POWER, Jan. / Feb., 1990 p. 15).

Executives manage by "walking around." Each officer is assigned a sales district and must spend time in the trenches learning what the customer wants and needs and what the sales force has to say and report. That alone would not have value, but the company stresses the need and importance of working together to improve programs and make them responsive to customer needs and "walks what it talks."

What does it talk? Well, according to Fred Smith, "The most important job of everyone at Federal Express is that we deliver a quality service 100% of the time, so that we achieve a 100% satisfied customer. Achieving this goal means that every member of the Federal Express team has to internalize the 29 performance standards. The first such standard is "Do it right the first time, no matter how insignificant the task may seem." This is important in any business, but particularly so in a business where one mistake triggers a domino effect which will/could abort the commitment to deliver packages to the customer before 10:30 a.m. To make certain that this domino pattern does not occur, the 1-10-100 rule (developed by Labovitz and Chang) is quoted over and over, "For every dollar your company might spend on preventing a quality problem, it will spend ten to inspect and correct the mistake after it occurs. In the worst case, the quality failure goes unchecked and unnoticed until after your customer has taken delivery. To fix the problem at this stage, you'll probably pay about one hundred times what you could have paid to prevent it from happening at all."

The crux of this view is that anything short of perfection is detrimental to the customer. We thought about this view, and decided it had real validity. Would you like a 99% perfect filling; a 99% perfect operation; a 99% safe airplane; or a 99% safe boat? True, the odds are in your favor, but is that enough? Shouldn't we make certain that all of our companies and organizations provide 100% perfect customer service?

The people who responded to our inquiries at Federal Express were delightful, and the one who has worked most closely with us, Shirley Finley at the Corporate Offices, went out of her way to make certain that our questions were answered thoroughly and accurately. The most impressive aspect of communication with the company was the obvious belief by everyone concerned that "it was their job!" This attitude was in marked contrast to a number of other employees at other "so-called" service oriented companies, even two who eventually shared very valuable data with us. In the latter two cases, we were delighted to finally find someone who truly did "own the call." Those individuals changed our negative perceptions and put us back into a belief mode about the exemplary nature of the two firms. One person can truly make the difference in customer attitude. This concept is well expressed by the following passage:

ARE "NICE CUSTOMERS" RUINING YOUR BUSINESS

I'm a nice customer. you all know me. I'm the one who never complains, no matter what kind of service I get.

I'll go into a restaurant and sit quietly while the waiters and waitresses gossip and never bother to ask if anyone has taken my order. Sometimes a party that came in after I did gets their order, but I don't complain. I just wait.

And when I go to a store to buy something. I don't throw my weight around. I try to be thoughtful of the other person. If a snooty salesperson gets upset because I want to look at several things before making up my mind, I'm just as polite as can be. I don't believe rudeness in return is the answer.

The other day I stopped at a full service gas station and waited for almost five minutes before the attendant took care of me. And when he did, he spilled gas and wiped the windshield with an oily rag. But did I complain about the service? Of course not.

I never kick. I never nag. I never criticize. And I wouldn't dream of making a scene, as I've seen some people do in public places. I think that's uncalled for. No, I'm a nice customer. And I'll tell you who else I am.

I'm the customer who
never comes back!

Author unknown

Employees at Federal Express and the customers of Federal Express profit from the points made in the 182 page Manager's Guide. The entire philosophy of the company is succinctly expressed in three letters **P-S-P (People-Service-Profits),** and it is the role of management to provide the leadership and culture which will enable customer contact employees to do their job. This means that those individuals need to be hired, trained, and paid to make the right decisions on the frontline, and then rewarded and recognized for their efforts.

The Manager's Guide presents guidelines for implementing the SQI (Service Quality Indicator) which was the outgrowth of the company's desire to more definitively measure service—both quantitatively and qualitatively. When research was begun, the company was already achieving a 98% level of service success. However, when 1.5 million packages are delivered per day, even 2% represents 30,000 shipments and customers. They wanted to figure out a system that would permit improvement even as package volume continued to increase. The SQI was the outgrowth. Fred Smith, the CEO, initially identified what he termed the Hierarchy of Horrors:

- wrong day delivery
- pickup not made
- lost package

- right day, late delivery
- misinformed customer
- billing or paperwork errors
- employee performance error
- damaged package.

Through this valuable information was gathered to help them improve systems and customer satisfaction, but more was needed.

Therefore, the SQI was "designed to reflect the customer's view of our performance by placing greater weight on those categories that have the greatest impact on the customers' perception of service received. New categories were added to those in the Hierarchy—aircraft delay minutes and abandoned calls were included in order to measure internal performance that can significantly affect external customer service. In addition, the SQI was designed to permit expansion and adjustment as needed, and the findings are tracked and reported on a weekly basis with monthly summaries. Although it is currently only used for Domestic deliveries, plans are underway to expand it to include International ones.

In addition to a training program which requires 4-5 weeks of training before any call is taken (and only then if the manager believes the person is able to perform effectively), recurrent training is a regular employment component, and interactive video instruction has been introduced. This program which standardizes information, provides flexibility, and individualization has been used to train some 7,000 CSAs and 24,000 couriers to date, and the 1,250 IVI units are in some 625 locations to facilitate their use. The result, better informed employees and a 60% reduction in training time.

Since the customer's satisfaction is the key to all corporate planning, the cardinal rule in the company is "to remain calm and treat the customer with the utmost respect." Staff is never to argue, make excuses, pass "the buck," instead no matter how angry the customer, he or she has a problem that the FEDEX employee is to solve. In order to do this most effectively, daily calls are made to customers to find out what they really want and think about the service, and focus groups and letters are a vital part of the feedback system.

In fact, it was this feedback that led to the purchase of the Flying Tigers. Customers wanted one-stop service, and FEDEX had a weight limit of 150 pounds, the solution, buy a airline that had no such limit!

Central to their success is teamwork, and that teamwork is evident in the Quality Action Teams which flourish throughout the company—they solve problems and work with departments to make a difference. Teams are rewarded for their success, and team spirit is easily spotted by looking at the T-shirts, mugs, banners, buttons, balloons, and acronyms that abound.

Individuals are rewarded, too, and the belief that individual achievement should be recognized has led to some interesting programs.

The Suggestion Awards Program encourages employees to

- present ideas on ways to lower costs,increase production and operating revenues, or

- promote safer working conditions.

When those ideas are implemented, the proposer is rewarded.

Turnover is the bane of many companies, but at FEDEX the longevity of the staff has led to a **Service Awards Program** which recognizes service and gives awards after every five years up to the 25th anniversary with the company.

To recognize teamwork and cooperation and work well done. the **Bravo Zulu program** was implemented. Extraordinary performance is recognized through both cash and noncash awards, and letters of appreciation are sent for admirable performance such as perfect attendance and no accidents.

The Golden Falcon Award is given to those whose service to customers (nominations are often based on unsolicited customer letters citing outstanding performance), and the winners are announced monthly through company publications and video programs. The winners receive a Golden Falcon lapel pin and shares of FEDEX common stock.

The Pay for Performance philosophy allows the company to pay employees for individual and or group performance. Merit programs, star/ superstar programs, MBO/MIC and PBO/ PIC programs and PRO PAY are in place and provide monetary rewards for those who accomplish and exceed corporate objectives and goals.

Awards are frequently awarded (Top 10 Business Triumphs of the 70's; One of 5 Best Managed Companies of 1981; One of the Ten Best Companies to Work For in America in 1985; A Great Place to Work, 1988; Marketing **Statesman** of the Year, 1989) to Federal Express, but the best reward is the confidence and satisfaction of its customers. There is no doubt in the minds of those who use the services of this company that the customer is always first.

THE LINE THAT SELLS SERVICE: DON'T LEAVE HOME WITHOUT IT

Service is the keystone of **American Express'** corporate philosophy, and the titles held by James Robinson attest to it.

He is both the CEO and the Chief Quality Officer—a fact that a member of his Public Relations staff says "illustrates that American Express' commitment to quality really starts at the top." The by-laws of the corporation support her view since they spell out the position as follows: "The Chief Quality Officer shall be the Chief Executive Officer of the corporation...[and] shall actively ensure that all employees...emphasize the consistent delivery of high quality service to the corporation's customers and employees."

Big business can still be responsive to its customers as American Express has continued to prove. In order to do this effectively, cardholders are segmented so that each can be served and targeted with a great deal of precision. According to FORTUNE (November 20, 1989) this company is a "money machine [which] keeps whirring." The article's author, John Paul Newport, Jr., went on to say that American Express "can serve as a model for companies struggling to figure out how to compete in the 1990's and beyond, [for] long before other U.S. corporations woke up to the importance of quality customer service, Amexco had taken it to heart."

This industry giant—it owns Shearson Lehman Hutton, Investors Diversified Services, and First Data Resources—now runs, in addition to its financial services and travel services, a direct marketing division that already sells "more consumer products through the mail than L.L. Bean and a publishing arm which is planning to create or acquire a dozen magazines. However, all of these companies have one common theme—their emphasis on service.

Management insists that employees strive to deliver the highest quality of service possible while anticipating and embracing change that will accelerate the focus on quality.

James D. Robinson III, CEO and Chief Quality Officer, whose patrician background insures his understanding of the carriage trade and the quality it demands, and he has used this understanding to better serve the mass market bank credit card customer. One of his slogans is, "Quality is the only patent protection we've got...The glue that binds all of this together is a commitment to quality in everything we do." It's what's gotten American Express where it is today, and it's the 'patent protection' that will keep us ahead of the curve of the future."

Such a goal demands on-going monitoring and management to insure that quality service is provided. Robinson, when he was head of what became the company's Travel Related Services (TRS) division, introduced a process of self-assessment which is still in use. As part of this, managers review

- phone response time of service center representatives (the average call is answered in three rings)

- card replacement time (the standard: 48 hours and 24 hour emergency card replacement)

- customer perception of service

- card processing time, and

- bill accuracy.

Since he believes that the delivery system is critical, whatever efficiency is introduced must be judged by how well it translates into better service that is **noticeable** to the customer. In order to insure that this happens, there is a standing board of managers from across the country whose job it is to develop new ways to measure and improve quality service. Periodic quality conferences are convened to devise ways to increase the company's competitive edge, and a Quality University provides line employees and managers with courses that build on the company's desire to and efforts to please its customers. Heroic mements in quality (i.e., the woman who delivered a card to a stranded traveler in the dead of night) are related in a series of Great Performers booklets which are distributed worldwide to some 45,000 employees. The award was instituted in 1982 as a means of recognizing employees who take the initiative to perform tasks that are clearly beyond their normal assignment. All full-time employees in the Travel Related Services Company below the level of director are eligible, and in all, more than a third of the 48,000 employees can participate. Selection for the award is based upon defined criteria, and it must be shown that the nominee has

- performed exceptional service that is clearly not within his or her job description.

- demonstrated unusual creativity or resourcefulness in assisting a customer.

- developed new ways or set new, higher

standards for the delivery of customer service.

- demonstrated extraordinary problem solving for a customer, especially when the task requires coordination among two or more American Express business units or divisions.

In an era where "everyone" has a credit card, the real skill that sets American Express apart from others is their ability to determine what card "members" want, and this is done through surveys, testing and marketing of new ideas and card enhancements (i.e., automatic car rental insurance and 24 hour customer service) and determining which ones appeal to which groups. How can they tailor something so general as a credit card service? By segmenting the card carrying universe into groups based on income and lifestyle characteristics and then presenting and publicizing the appropriate services to each.

Many companies would be happy to sit still and reap the profits from this effective marketing strategy, but not Robinson who feels that change is inevitable, so they need to shape it or take advantage of it. In other words, his staff is asked to listen, read, analyze, respond, and plan around the data that is available to them. According to Raymond J. Larkin in a presentation entitled, "The History of Quality at American Express" in 1987, Jim Robinson's response to concerned staff stepping forward with a viable plan of action was SUPPORT. In this speech, Larkin pointed out that Jim Robinson says that the "company's success depends on four factors: quality, quality, quality, and quality." He went on to note that "while quality assurance...began as a way to ensure consistent delivery" of their services, they found that its benefits far surpassed the original objectives. He noted that this goal

- had more sharply focused "the attention of the entire company where it belongs, on the customer;

- had improved productivity; had contributed millions to the bottom line;

- had built up employee morale and pride; had proven to be an investment of money and people which has paid them back over and over again;

- had continued to give the company the competitive edge in the marketplace."

In 1978, a decision was made to launch a new quality assurance methodology to track, evaluate and correct weak spots in service delivery. A presentation was made to senior management, and within "one minute of finishing our presentation, Jim Robinson said to me, 'Ray, you have three quarters of a million dollars. You have half a million to spend now, then come to me when you need the rest. But start immediately,' With that financial support, quality assurance was on its way."

Such concern for customers is not limited to the credit card division. After acquiring IDS and tapping into the savings and investment market, American Express stressed to their new division and its 6,000 financial planners/representatives, the importance of "getting to know your customers.'".

Each of these 6,000 reps is encouraged to follow the corporate philosophy—"promise only what you can deliver and then deliver more than you promised." The entire management process might not work with a less secure CEO, for Robinson supports and encourages his strong-willed subordinates whose blunt responses and comments are given serious consideration. In fact, he has been heard to say, "People are the biggest risk I have," but he knows that the axiom "Whatever you did yesterday to get you where you are today, may not be sufficient to to keep you there tomorrow" is true.

The concept isn't new, but it is only those companies that endorse change, input, and strive for excellence in customer service that can expect to move to or stay in the forefront in the next decade. In fact in a Gallup Poll conducted in 1987, 48% of the senior executives in the 615 companies polled indicated that in the next three years service quality would be the most important factor to consider and "offering their customers better service [would] be nearly as important as making higher quality products." The staff at AmEx agrees, and according to 2/3 of the board of advisors for Marketer of the Year Award sponsored by CREDIT CARD MANAGEMENT, "[American Express} delivers on services."

This means that quality must be stressed, service given, and change fostered in order to serve the customers (there are 33.7 million American Express cards in force worldwide). Spencer Nilson who writes a credit card industry newsletter said, "There's no getting around the fact that American Express' service is far and away the best in the industry."

Many companies are unwilling to make the initial investment needed to insure that effective, interactive service is possible.

Such service requires extensive training for its customer service representatives. American Express provides six to eight weeks of such training for its service specialists many of whom are drawn from other areas of the company.   Such training and interactive service pays off in fewer complaints, easier marketing, and new product development as well as the bottom line—profits.

At the heart of all of these systems is enlightened planning for corporate success. This sensitivity to customers and their concerns dates back to the early 80's and Ruth C. Finley (who although no longer with the company was a regional vice president of the Card Division) indicated that she believed that customers were most concerned about three things" timeliness, accuracy, and responsiveness in fulfiling their requests (it is very likely that a similar study would produce identical results now)." She expressed the view that is still held at American Express, "Customers do not think of themselves as numbers. To them, their card is one of a kind." (<u>AMA Forum</u>, March 1962) One of American Express' executives once said, "In the old days, the mom-and-pop stores knew their customers intimately, and instinctively matched their service to each customer...That's what we're trying to do—run AmEx's service like a huge mom-and-pop drugstore." They do and it works!

EVERY MOMENT IS A MOMENT OF TRUTH AT SAS

No study of outstanding customer service would be complete without reference to **Scandinavian Airlines Systems (SAS)** and its CEO. The fact that this is so is due to the skillful leadership of its CEO, Jan Carlzon, who in 1981 took over a company on the verge of losing $20 million and by 1982 led a company earning $54 million.

What triggered this unprecedented change? Carlzon, who insists that a successful service business must be customer-driven, capitalized on what he called the 50,000 "moments of truth" each day—the moments when customers come into contact with the company.

His success has been noted by colleagues, authors, and competitors. A number have even brought him into their companies to share the insight and system that has been termed "a prescription for corporate leadership" by R. L. Crandall, Chairman and President of AMR and American Airlines. Mr. Crandall pointed out that Carlzon recognizes the importance of "responding to a changing marketplace, focuses on the "importance of the activist manager, "and the necessity for "forcing decision making down to the corporate cutting edge."

With these points in mind and having recently read his well-received book, MOMENTS OF TRUTH, we contacted SAS and asked if they would share some key tips with us. Mr. Bert Stromberg, based in Stolkholm and Director of Customer Relations, graciously did so, and set forth below are the guidelines that have made SAS an international force in the airline industry.

SAS operates under a principle mentioned numerous times in this book—**LISTEN and LEARN.** Listen to your customers, analyze their problems or concerns, find a way to help them resolve or solve them, and learn from what was heard and done. Then take the steps needed to insure that others do not have to walk the same path.

In order to make certain that this happens on a consistent basis, it is vital that **active consumer research** be an on-going process which **gathers and follows-up** on passengers' view points.

Once this information is on hand pull down those invisible barriers—the barriers that may well block action and change—and take action. In fact, if possible **settle issues or take action on the spot,** when it is needed. When this is done the patrons know you care and know that you are truly involved in making certain that the company serves them effectively and with a serious concern for their needs and wants. Remember "by treating each customer as an individual, and by always putting the customer in focus in all situations" everyone is given "the feeling that we are all involved and can take necessary action as needed."

All of these goals mean that management has a crucial role. Members of the management team must understand the corporate mission, understand how they fit into the picture, and be able to provide straightforward, clear information to both the customers and staff. This means that guidelines must be clear, and management must be "management by love, not fear." This means that the traditional pyramid must be flattened with responsibility and authority being married and put into the hands of those who have the direct contact with customers since "service and the frontline people who deliver it [are] the success levers.

In this market driven era, Carlzon contents that "the customer oriented company [must be] organized for change." This means that "horizontal barriers to communication" must disappear and the frontline people kept informed. Act, don't become bogged down in analysis, instead honor "emotion, intuition, and showmanship, " but remember to set high standards. "People shine only if demands are sky high."

Since this is the case, he believes that staff is the true foundation of any company. "If you ask our customers about SAS, they won't tell you about our planes or our offices or the way finance our capital investments. Instead, they'll talk about their experiences with the people at SAS." This means that we "cannot rely on rule books and instructions from distant corporate offices. We have to place responsibility for ideas, decisions, and actions with the people who **are** SAS during those 15 seconds—ticket agents, flight attendances, baggage handlers, and all other frontline employees." As you can see, Carlzon literally turns that corporate pyramid upside down. Actually, at Linjeflyg he turned it into the shape of a heart. One half of the heart generated revenue and the other half incurred expenses, and the theme song he introduced with his changes was "Love Is in the Air." With his changes and the information he shared with employees came a new dedication to the job, and although people worked hard, they did it by choice, and many indicated that they hadn't had as much fun in years!

He did not throw out analysis, but he did redirect it. With his staff he scrutinizes every resource, every expense, every procedure, and asks if it is needed to better serve. If they do, they strive to improve it; if they don't, they jettison it; if they don't have it, they prepare to add it. The importance of making decisions is stressed not the need to be cautious and make no errors. In fact, Carlzon believes that "mistakes can usually be corrected later, [but] the time lost in not making a decision can never be retrieved."

The resultant delegation of authority means that on-going communication is necessary, for "anyone who is not given information cannot assume responsibility." One of the most delightful stories shared by Carlzon in his book MOMENTS OF TRUTH exemplifies this view. "Now I intend to take a four weeks' vacation," I stated. "If my telephone doesn't ring, that is proof that I have succeeded—people have accepted responsibility and are making decisions on their own. But if the phone rings, then I have failed—either to get my message across or in recruiting managers who can accept responsibility." During his four week vacation, the phone never rang—his approach succeeded.

Although some managers equate delegation with abdication, that is not the case. Each level of the corporate structure needs to coach, inform, criticize, praise, educate, and work with the levels above and below them to implement the overall corporate strategies and mobilize the needed resources needed to insure success.

The success of a company can only be unleashed when the energy of a blended, enthusiastic team understands and "buys into" the corporation's guiding vision.

When that happens, when employees can understand the role they are playing within the structure of the corporate mission, they no longer see the service they render as an isolated incident but rather as an important part of a "big picture." Carlzon expresses it beautifully when he tells about two stone cutters each chipping square blocks out of granite. When asked what they were doing, the first grumbled sourly, "I'm cutting this damned stone into a block." The other who seemed to be pleased with his work, replied with pride, "I'm on the team that's building a cathedral." The first saw only a block of granite, the other a cathedral for the ages. Who do you think put more into his work and provided better for the ultimate user? In order to insure that the moments of truth in your company produce a lasting masterpiece of customer service, it is necessary for the leaders to determine the design, share it, and then inspire those who must build it.

PEOPLE ARE THEIR
MOST IMPORTANT ASSET

After hearing from other corporate leaders, we were not surprised to learn tht Bill Tiefel, President of the **Marriott Corporation,** told those attending a national conference for CEOs in October of 1989 that "people are our most important asset. We're convinced there is no way we can sustain any competitive advantage we might have in the marketplace with pretty buildings. That our people are everything to us goes to the very heart of our way of thinking and doing business."

He went on to tell those present that they believed in treating their employees "the way we want them to treat our customers." In order to do this

- their 230,000 associates are provided with every avenue to success.

- we ask their opinion and listen to and act on their suggestions.

- we empower them to take action without having to check SOPs (standard operating procedures) when dealing with a guest.

- we strive to know a little bit about their aspirations and ambitions.

- we try to provide them with opportunities to reach their full potential.

- we provide a shopping list of benefits including profit sharing and preferential employee stock purchasing opportunities.

- we provide the training that makes the difference since well trained, motivated associates enjoy their jobs more and provide more effectively for our guests. Therefore, we allot substantial monies, time, and effort to training for all employees geared to their job level needs.

Using Carlzon's formula, the Marriott and their associates have over 25 million "moments of truth" each day, and their business fails or succeeds "one customer at a time." This means that they must continue to **ask and learn.** A few years ago, they even produced a video depicting actual interviews with guests and asking them to share their best and their worst experiences while at a Marriott hotel. This video was then used as a part of one of their training programs, an OPTS Program on hospitality designed by the authors.

The concerns expressed at that time have in many instances been handled and the suggested changes implemented. This concentration on meeting customer needs and expectations not only serves the customer well, it is also good business. It costs five times more money to attract new customers than to keep an old one, so it isn't surprising to learn that the changes noted below were the outgrowth of customer comments:

- breakfasts are delivered in five minutes or are free.

- video checkouts have been added to help business travelers avoid long checkout lines.

- fitness facilities have been put in all of their hotels menus have been revised to incorporate foods for the health conscious guests.

According to Tiefel, "the secret of good service rests with providing what our guests believe good service to be." Has this philosophy paid off? You bet it did. Sixty two years ago the Marriott family opened a nine seat root beer stand, 32 years ago they opened their first hotel; and in 1989, they opened their 500th hotel in Warsaw, Poland. So what is best for the customers is also obviously best for the company.

CLASSICAL MANAGEMENT VS. FUNCTIONAL MANAGEMENT OF CUSTOMER SERVICE

Experts have long extolled those in management to plan effectively, organize efficiently, motivate appropriately, and thereby lead skillfully. As you can see from the comments made by those who have led their companies to financial success, they believe that innovative managers have a high People Quotient. They care about others—what they think and how they feel; they share both responsibilities and authority with their subordinates and colleagues; they believe in, and understand the concept of internal and external customer service. They realize that the corporate team can make successful customer service a repeatable experience, for people support what they create. It is up to you to know your customer, create your strategy, plan with your staff right down to the grass roots, set the standards of excellence and then create a service culture that insures that the values, norms, beliefs, and ideologies of your company are focused **on service.**

KEY STRATEGY #21

SERVICE IS A TWO SIDED COIN, SERVE THE CUSTOMER WELL, AND YOU WILL AUTOMATICALLY BEST SERVE THE COMPANY.

22

INSIDER
ANECDOTES

The Unique Company finds out
what customers want and need
and then provide it.

Don Smith
Vice President—Sales/Marketing
Affiliated Foods

Months of research provided us with valuable systems and techniques for ensuring the development and implementation of an effective customer service program. In addition, there was a bonus upon which we never planned, a rich reservoir of anecdotes that tell the story of customer service as no narrative can. These true stories illustrate the real meaning of customer service—caring enough to try uncharted waters, going the "extra mile," and making unprecedented decisions on the spot.

DEFUSING ANGRY CUSTOMERS

A well-known speaker was staying at a Hyatt while presenting a program at a nearby company. When she arrived, she was put into a room that did not fit the requests made at the time it was reserved. In addition, there was a problem with the registration itself; a guaranteed reservation had somehow been misplaced. Tired, frustrated, and more than a little put out, she finally got registered and into a room—one that didn't really suit her. She called down and told the manager the problems encountered. He listened quietly and expressed his apologies. Fifteen minutes later, room service delivered a beautiful fruit basket and a hand written note from the manager apologizing and letting her know that everyone was there to serve her and help make certain that her stay was a pleasant one.

Digital Equipment Corporation based in Colorado Springs has a nationwide has 24 hour customer service program. Recently a frustrated customer placed a call to this center, and slowly calmed down as he learned that the person who took the call "owned the call." She listened to him as he explained his problem, made all the contacts necessary to secure answers, relayed them, made the necessary arrangements to have the problem corrected, and stayed with him right through to the solution. He was "her" customer and she made certain that the resolution made him happy.

INNOVATIVE SERVICE

Recently, a Los Angeles based consulting firm wanted to say "thank you" to the employees of Community Press, a Provo, Utah, based printing company by having lunch catered for them. A call was placed to Richard Bandley, owner/manager of **Kentucky Fried Chicken** in Spanish Fork. Together a menu was worked out and arrangements made to have the food delivered in time for the staff to gather for a holiday celebration. Despite the fact that everything had to be arranged by phone and fax, all went smoothly because one person took the time to work with the customer.

The clerk at **Jorgenson's** market in Pasadena learned that one of the long time customers had just died. On his own initiative, he called to find out what time the family would be returning from the graveside and told the person answering when a catered meal would arrive. He worked with the staff and assembled platters of cold cuts and fresh vegetables. When the family returned to the house, the dining room table was beautifully set out, and a note from the store staff expressed their sorrow at the family's loss and and their desire to help in any way they could. The family was astounded because no one had ordered the buffet. When they called the store, they were even more shocked, for they learned that it was a gift from the store employees.

Dusty's Floral Shop has impressed a number of people in the past few years by the extra effort shown by staff. At a funeral held in December of 1988, the staff took all out-of-town orders and very carefully planned the floral arrangements so that no two were the same. In another instance, a call was taken from someone who wanted some help with birthday wishes for her parents. The customer was out of town, but she wanted to make certain that her Mother knew she was remembered. She asked that a floral arrangement be created in her Mother's favorite colors and mentioned the birthday. She then asked if the florist knew of a good bakery and could give her the name. To her amazement, the employee volunteered to arrange for the cake, get some balloons, and deliver all three things to the Mother's house that afternoon. She did just that, paid for the cake and balloons and then put the items on the floral bill.

In 1989, one of **Land's End** mail order customers was ill and confined to his bed. Too ill to shop for Christmas presents, he was at his wits end when he decided to call Land's End and see what could be done. Using his catalogue and the services of a truly patient order clerk, he worked with her to pick out suitable presents for the people on his holiday list. In addition to the hour she spent with him on the phone, the CSR arranged to have all of the presents delivered in time for Christmas. The patience and concern she showed made such an impression that the man has since shared the story with dozens of friends.

Families of those needing intensive care are under tremendous pressure and strain, yet all too often the very busy staffs at hospitals find little time to consider these "customers" and their pressing needs. Such was not the case in 1988 when a family gathered at **Stevens Hospital** in Edmonds, Washington, to stand vigil beside a seriously ill and dearly loved mother, grandmother, and wife. Each evening, one of the nurses would come by and fix up a bed for the husband so that he could spend the night beside his wife, bring blankets to the daughter and grandchildren so that they could sleep in the lounge since all were anxious to remain nearby.

The concern and love given to the woman and her family by the staff and doctor helped them through a traumatic period of their lives, and they were truly touched to look up at the funeral and find a number of the nursing staff present at the services for this woman so dear to them but known to the hospital personnel for only three weeks.

CREATIVE SOLUTIONS

Both authors have experienced unique service above and beyond the call of duty from **Kelly Services.** At different times and in different cities each had a Kelly Person fail to appear to help with registrations. Calls were made to the local office, and much to their surprise in each case, the managers of the local offices rushed over to handle registrations and general clerical duties for the morning. In each case, the managers, both women, indicated that a commitment had been made and had to be kept.

When equipment breaks down many companies shrug, apologize and take no responsibility for the resultant delays. This is not the way **AT & T** handled a 1990 breakdown in service which affected the Eastern Seaboard. The disruption of service lasted 5 hours, and as a way of apologizing for the inconvenience it caused, the company made discounted service (holiday rates) available to all of its customers on Valentine's Day.

Another telephone company employee—**Southern Bell's**--was lauded in her company newspaper for service that involved many facets of caring. An elderly man's family called to ask how they could arrange for service when he had limited funds but was a diabetic and needed immediately to be able to make contact in case of an emergency. The woman listened to the problem, arranged for the hook-up without a deposit, cut orders to immediate installation, and put the family in contact with agencies that could be of assistance to the man and to them. For her concern and efforts, she was honored by the company and blessed by the family.

Dedicated employees are the real "glue" (pardon the play on words) at **H. B. Fuller** (the largest independent adhesive company in the world). A few years ago a picture of Lorinda Tucker appeared in a company report which noted that she had truly gone beyond any level that could be expected of those in customer service. While her boss was out of the country, a call came in to Lorinda, a secretary at H.B. Fuller, and the customer anxiously shared his concerns. He was not locally based and he was running out of the glue he was using. She asked some questions and learned that he was not using one of their glues. Nevertheless, she took action, called another division in another state asked for help from one of their technical support people who figured out which of their 7000 adhesives would work and got back to her with the information. She took her own pick up out, picked up the needed supplies, drove to the airport only to learn that the company did not have an account with the air freight company. They wouldn't ship without their fee— $300, so she rushed to a automatic teller, withdrew $300 of her own money, returned, paid the bill, got the shipment off, and the customer suffered no downtime. In fact, the new adhesive worked far better than the old one.

There is no one blueprint for success, but there is no question about the fact that there is a customer revolution underway. Customers are demanding not only competitive prices, but also better service and greater convenience. Motivated staff, managers who move out of the executive suite and into the trenches, and executives who set the pace and the pattern can make a major difference. People are not widgets, and they don't want to be treated like widgets. When we remember that, we have taken a major step toward world class service.

KEY STRATEGY #22

TREAT YOUR CUSTOMERS AS YOU WOULD AN HONORED GUEST.

APPENDIX

THE CUSTOMER'S BILL OF RIGHTS

Every customer has the right to be served by those who have put into practice the following principles of good customer relations.

1. THE MORE YOU KNOW ABOUT THE PERSON WITH WHOM YOU ARE DEALING THE MORE EFFECTIVE YOU ARE GOING TO BE.

    Each person is unique and wants to be treated as a special individual. The better you understand them, the more effectively you can meet their needs and match their style and pace.

2. SUCCESS DEMANDS OPENING UP YOUR SENSES, TALKNG LESS AND LISTENING MORE.

    Make a game of matching your words to the listening language—visual, auditory, or feeling—of your customers. It can be fun, and is certainly effective.

3. THOSE WHO DEAL MOST EFFEC-
TIVELY WITH CUSTOMERS OR
CLIENTS ARE THOSE WHO "PARK
THEIR EGO AT THE DOOR."

Forget about yourself and treat your customers as they need to be treated.

4. REMEMBER THAT YOUR CON-
SCIOUS AND UNCONSCIOUS ARE
THE BASIS FOR THE RELATION-
SHIPS YOU FORM WITH CUSTOM-
ERS AND COLLEAGUES.

When you communicate, are your words
matched by your body language?

5. THERE IS NO EXCUSE FOR "ALMOST
RIGHT."   CUSTOMERS HAVE THE
RIGHT TO EXPECT "RIGHT."

Customers and clients pay for expert help
and good products, and they deserve both.

6. PROMISES BROKEN ARE BUSINESS
LOST.

Do you keep your word? Every cent that
flows through a company comes from the

clients/customers. You have a job as long as they are satisfied.

7. PATIENCE PAYS DIVIDENDS.

    Invest patience in your customers and clients; the return on that investment is literally your livelihood.

8. REMEMBER THAT ONLY THOSE WHO DO NOTHING NEVER MAKE MISTAKES.

    TRY to do it right, but if you make a mistake, admit it.

9. CUSTOMERS ARE NOT INTERRUP-TIONS BUT INCENTIVES.

    Business is a game, and you need to know the rules, follow them, and play to win.

10. A SMILE HAS NO VALUE UNTIL YOU SHARE IT.

    Remember, we are all customers, and a smile can make a major difference in our day, our feelings, and our reactions to you and your service or product.

11. EVERYONE GETS ANGRY. IT'S HOW YOU DEAL WITH IT THAT MATTERS!

Remember, we all must deal with irate customers. Solving the problem will bring customer satisfaction.

12. TAKE A POWER POSITION AND THEN NEGOTIATE FOR A WIN/WIN SOLUTION!

Remember not to let others write the "rules of your game," but don't forget that everyone needs to feel a successful part of the negotiation.

13. STEP OUT OF YOUR BOX. TAKE A CREATIVE APPROACH TO YOUR JOB.

Remember to developing your creativity so you can to see solutions which others miss.

14. PACKAGE FOR SUCCESS, IMAGE MAKES THE DIFFERENCE.

Remember you have only four minutes to make an impression. Make sure you are projecting the correct image.

15. RETURN STRESS TO ITS RIGHTFUL OWNER. YOU TAKE CONTROL.

   Remember to recognize the symptoms of stdress which can lead to burn-out.

16. CHANGE IS A CONSTANT WITH WHICH WE HAVE TO LIVE AND TO WHICH WE HAVE TO ADJUST!

   Remember to view change as a challenge not a threat!

17. MANAGEMENT SETS THE TONE: STAFF IMPLEMENTS IT!

   Remember that successful managers keep their sense of humor, master communication skills, and are flexible and creative.

18. THE RIGHT STAFF CHOICES CAN MAKE THE DIFFERENCE IN CUSTOMER RELTIONS.

   Remember, we tend to hire by experience, skills, personal projection, and recommendations, but we fire for behaviors!

19. ORGANIZATION THAT WELCOME CHANGE AND ACCEPT REALITIES FIND THEMSELVES GAINING THE COMPETITIVE EDGE.

Remember, the most important people in any company are the people who interact directly with the customer. Prepare them to respond to changing situations as if they were opportunities, not problems.

20. CUSTOMER SERVICE IS THE MAGIC FORMULA FOR SUCCESS IN ANY INDUSTRY

Remember, worry about what is best for the customer, and what is best for the company will automatically follow.

21. SERVICE IS A TWO SIDED COIN, SERVE THE CUSTOMER WELL, AND YOU WILL AUTOMATICALLY BEST SERVE THE COMPANY.

Remember, it is up to you to set the standards of excellence and then create a service culture that insures that the values, norms, beliefs, and ideologies of your company are focused **on service.**

22. TREAT YOUR CUSTOMERS AS YOU WOULD AN HONORED GUEST.

Remember, people want to be treated with respect and receive individual attention

KEY STRATEGIES

There are a number of strategies that can be used to solve little problems before they escalate into big ones. Remember, you CAN solve disputes, "smooth ruffled feathers", and defuse stressful situations when you couple these strategies with skill, tact, and patience.

	STRATEGY TACTIC		IMPACT
1.	Empathize and show that you want to help, not confront	1.	Defuse antagonism
2.	Demonstrate interest	2.	Establishes rapport
3.	Keep your won emotions in check	3.	Calms others down
4.	Probe tactfully for details	4.	Uncovers the "real" problem
5.	Concentrate on the problem, not the person	5.	Reduces tensions
6.	Use words that produce cooperation, not confrontation	6.	Improves interaction
7.	Decide who should handle the problem	7.	Puts the problem with the decision-makers
8.	Act promptly and decisively	8.	Gains customer acceptance

STRATEGY	TACTIC
9. Make the customer your partner in the decision	9. What we "own," we support
10. Emphasize the benefits of the solution	10. Provides positive reinforcement
11. Develop standard operating procedures for handling complaints or suggestions	11. Provides consistency and maximizes effort
12. Let management know about complaints and solutions/effort made	12. Supports the team approach for long-term planning
13. Encourage customers and clients to make suggestions related to service, needs, products, and approaches	13. Insures a match

As you can see from this strategy chart, you must be able to play many roles in order to succeed in customer relations.

YOU NEED TO LISTEN TO THE WORDS, RECOGNIZE NEEDS, AND USE THE APPROPRIATE APPROACH AND LANGUAGE IF YOU WANT TO COMMUNICATE.

YOU NEED TO BE BOTH A PACIFIER AND A NEGOTIATOR WITH CUSTOMER CONSCIOUSNESS IF YOU WANT TO INSURE CUSTOMER LOYALTY.

YOU NEED TO BE BOTH A PROBLEM SOLVER AND AN EXPEDITOR IF YOU WANT TO REDUCE THE IMPACT OF CUSTOMER COMPLAINTS.

YOU NEED TO BE ABLE TO SPOT IN-HOUSE PROBLEMS IF YOU WANT TO OFFSET POTENTIAL PROBLEMS.

When you use these strategies, you can cope more effectively with customer problems which fall into the following categories:

- misunderstandings
- delays
- wrong merchandise
- product quality
- wrong information
- poor service
- behavioral conflicts
- price disputes
- credit problems

SALES APPROACH TO PERSONALITY STYLE No. 1

LEADER	PERSUADER	INDEPENDENT
Quick Decision	Quick Decision	Quick Decision
Short Attention Span	Short Attention Span	Short Attention Span
Wants Results	Wants Recognition	Wants Action
Few Questions/No Small Talk	Loves Stories with Triumph/Disaster	New Horizons and Adventure
Hard Hitting/Driver	Enthusiastic/ Energetic	Own Person/ Excitement
Task Oriented	People Oriented	Action Oriented
Relevant Humor Only	People Humor	Status Humor
Maintain Poker Face	Visual/Lots of Props	Involved/To the Point
Be Efficient	Be warm	Be the Best
Likes Forceful Points	Likes Emotion and Drama	Likes a Different Approach
Time Factor Important	Excitement Factor Important	Quality Factor IImportant
Hates Details	Hates Boring People/Ideas	Hates Restraints
Approach to You: Efficient/Impatient	Approach to You: Warm/Host	Approach to You: Hurried/Challenging
Needs Authority	Needs to Help Others	Needs New Horizons
Wants: Direct Answer	Wants: Recognition	Wants: Excitement/ Action
Influenced by Force Freedom of Character	Influenced by Invitation and Persuasion	Influenced by of Ideas and Action
Wants Immediate Results	Wants to Look Good and Gain Approval	Wants No Restrictions and No Control
Close: Fast	Close:With Emotional Turn-On	Close: With a Flourish

SALES APPROACH TO PERSONALITY STYLE No. 2

PATIENT	CAREFUL	RESERVED
Slow Decision	Slow Decision	Slow Decision
Long Attention Span	Long Attention Span	Long Attention Span
Low Pressure	Low Pressure	Low Pressure
Down to Earth Presentation	Credentials/Facts Presentation	Clearly Stated Presentation
Wants: All Questions Answered	Wants: Constant Reassurance	Wants: No Conflicts
Kindly Humor only!	No Humor	Quiet/Dry Humor
Be Sincere	Be Precise	Be Quiet
Likes Referrals	Likes Facts	Likes Methodology
You Must Fit into the Environment	You Must NOT Be Showy	You Must Be Relaxed
Hates Pressure	Hates Inaccuracy	Hates Loud or Bold
Approach to You: Careful/Screened	Approach to You: Fact-Finding Host	Approach to You: Apprehensive Hesitant
Influenced By Consistency	Influenced By Sense of Accuracy	Influenced By Security Clear-cut Directions
Doesn't Like Change	Limited Change	Will Implement/Some-time
Wants a Controlled Environment	Wants a Secure Environment	Wants a Peaceful Environment
Needs to Be Appreciated	Needs Structure	Needs Ideas and Concepts
Needs: Reassurance	Needs: Constant Support	Needs: Appreciation
Close: Slowly/Patiently	Close: With Facts and Figures	Close: Carefully and Very Supportingly

SALES STRATEGIES

IF YOU CAN'T CLOSE THE SALE, YOU'RE **A PROFESSIONAL VISITOR.**

There are five decisions a buyer makes before buying, all buying decisions are made in this order:

YOU

THE COMPANY

THE PRODUCT

PRICE

TIME

The system you need is one that follows these buying decisions.

SELL YOURSELF

FIND THE NEED

AGREE ON THE NEED

FILL THE NEED

CLOSE THE SALE

To be a professional, you must serve the needs and deal with the "I," not the masses. Learn to empathize with your client and develop an awareness based on intuition, wisdom, and knowledge.

(Learn to tailor your sales approach to the styles of the clients and customers for the greatest success.)

AN INVITATION FROM THE AUTHORS

We would love to hear about your approach to CUSTOMER RELATIONS. If your company or organization is doing something unusual, or particularly successful, please tell us about it.

If you would like to have a full-sized copy of the CUSTOMER'S BILL OF RIGHTS, please send us a self-addressed, stamped envelope. We will be glad to send it to you with our compliments.

If you are planning a meeting or convention and need speakers who can motivate your staff to greater productivity or can design and customer tailor a training program for you, please call us at (213) 822-3751. Thank you.

Elizabeth I. Kearney
Michale Joan Bandley
KEARNEY/BANDLEY ENTERPRISES
563 Washington Street
Marina del Rey, CA 90291

Kearney/Bandley Professional Series

Customers Run Your Company: They Pay The Bills

This book targets the needs of the 90's by giving you the strategies that attract, keep, and win back customers.

$12.95

Everyone Is A Customer

With this book you can build communication and motivational bridges. Read it and then duplicate the winning strategies.

$12.95

People Power: Reading People For Results

Use this guide to take the guesswork out of communication and interaction. "Read" people and **know** what they want.

$12.95

MLM Is Big Business: Fact Not Fiction

This book unlocks the secrets and shares the strategies of direct sales "giants."

$12.95

SEND IMMEDIATELY

563 Washington Street, Marina del Rey, CA 90291 (213) 822-3751

Name: _____ Title: _____ Date: _____

Company: _____ Phone: _____

Address: _____

	City	State	ZIP

#	Item	Price
___	Customers Run Your Business (book)	$12.95
___	Everyone is a Customer (book)	$12.95
___	Real Estate Match (book)	$12.95
___	Audio Synopsis of Everyone is a Customer	$9.95
___	People Power (book)	$12.95
___	Solid Gold Customer Relations (hardback)	$16.95
___	The Hidden Side of Customer Relations (tapes)	$59.95
___	How to Increase Your Real Estate Sales (tapes)	$59.95
___	Quality Starts With Management (video)	$39.95
___	Reading the Jury For Results (video)	$89.95
___	Brain Check (IBM compatible disk)	$59.95
___	Prospect Check (IBM compatible disk)	$59.95
___	People Check (IBM compatible disk)	$59.95

Sub Total _____

Add $2.50 per book for postage _____

CA residents add 7% sales tax _____

Total _____

Total enclosed: _____

Check enclosed $ _____

Bill:☐   VISA ☐   MC ☐

Card # _____

Expiration Date: _____

Signature: _____

Purchase Order # _____

° Call for special rates on large orders!

SEND INFORMATION ON:

☐ PresentationTopics
☐ Consulting Services
☐ Hiring/Training Tools
☐ Training Services